Piagetian Research

Volume One

PIAGETIAN RESEARCH:
Compilation and Commentary

Volume One

Jean Piaget: An appreciation and Piaget's major works
The theory of cognitive development
Sensorimotor intelligence

Sohan Modgil, PhD and Celia Modgil, MPhil

Foreword by Professor Bärbel Inhelder
The University of Geneva

NFER Publishing Company Ltd

Published by the NFER Publishing Company Ltd.,
2 Jennings Buildings, Thames Avenue,
Windsor, Berks. SL4 1QS
Registered Office: The Mere, Upton Park, Slough, Berks. SL1 2DQ
First Published 1976
© Sohan and Celia Modgil
ISBN 0 85633 089 2

Typeset by Jubal Multiwrite Ltd.,
66 Loampit Vale, London SE13 7SN
Printed in Great Britain by
Staples Printers Ltd., Rochester, Kent
Distributed in the USA by Humanities Press Inc.,
Hillary House—Fernhill House, Atlantic Highlands,
New Jersey 07716 USA.

Contents

FOREWORD   7

PREFACE   9

INTRODUCTION   11

Part One Jean Piaget   15
  a. An appreciation   17
  b. Piaget's major works   25

Part Two Theory of Cognitive Development   33
  a. Introduction   35
  b. Sensorimotor stage   37
  c. Pre-operational stage   39
  d. Stage of concrete operations   41
  e. Stage of formal operations   44
  f. General criticisms   47
  g. Interpretations and extensions   55
  h. Applications to education   64
  Abstracts   69

Part Three Sensorimotor Intelligence   103
  a. Introduction and related studies   105
  b. The concept of object permanence   113
  c. The development of object permanence in animals 125
  Abstracts   126

ABBREVIATIONS USED IN THE BIBLIOGRAPHY   151

BIBLIOGRAPHY   155

AUTHOR INDEX   168

To Gita and Kush-Luv

With Love

FOREWORD

I most sincerely thank Dr Sohan and Celia Modgil for asking me to write a foreword to the series of eight volumes which they are at present compiling. We all know the interest that was shown in, and the success of, the previous book, *Piagetian Research: A Handbook of Recent Studies*. Now, two years later, eight follow-up volumes are being published. We are well aware of what this represents in terms of continuity and devotion to such a long-term task.

The rapid extension of Piaget-inspired research is very impressive; in this series 3700 references are mentioned. It would seem that such an extension is explained by the need for a general theory in fundamental psychology. Another possible explanation is the growing awareness of the gaps in strictly behaviourist theory, on the one hand, and on the other, the continued emergence of new applications for the work carried out in Geneva in the fields of education and psychopathology. Recent studies confirm this trend.

Pleasing though this extension is, however, we are somewhat disturbed by the fact that the replication of our experiments does not always show a sufficient understanding of Piagetian theory on the part of the authors of these new works. We are of course the first to admit that such understanding is not easy to acquire, especially since this form of psychology is closely linked to a certain form of epistemology. Once understood, this form of epistemology appears to be that which best suits genetic psychology, as both are essentially constructivist. Constructivism implies that knowledge is not acquired merely under the impact of empirical experience, as suggested by behaviourist theory, although of course such impact is not entirely excluded from the process. It is also opposed to innate theory, to which, it seems, recourse is frequently had today (maturation being a factor which intervenes, but not exclusively). Constructivism emphasizes the child's or the subject's activity during the course of cognitive development: in other words, everything derives from actions and is eventually translated into coherent and logical thought operations.

In order to promote the necessary understanding, Sohan and Celia Modgil have systematically encouraged the reader to return to the original texts. If authors who have an excellent knowledge of the work of Piaget and his colleagues slightly misunderstand our theoretical position — which is in no way maturationist but rather epigenetic — one can easily imagine the misunderstanding of researchers who are less well informed and further away from Geneva. It is one thing to recognize the necessary sequence of the stages, but another thing altogether to explain them by invoking an innate 'programme'. Piaget's explanation, which is best presented in constructivist terms, deals with the sequence of stages by a process of equilibration or autoregulation. This regulatory activity enables the subject truly to construct knowledge — something which simple maturation does not do.

This point of view is fundamental to the understanding of Piagetian psychology; but more than that, it seems to us to constitute a particularly useful approach to questions of educational application since this form of autoconstruction corresponds more than any other perspective to the ideal called 'the active school', an ideal rarely carried out in practice.

In a constructivist perspective of this kind, it is clearly the sequence of stages which is important and not the chronological ages; the latter vary considerably from one environment to another and also depend on the experimental procedures being used. It is not astonishing that Bryant obtains convservation responses at earlier ages than those noted by us: we ourselves have obtained notable accelerations using operatory learning procedures developed in collaboration with H. Sinclair and M. Bovet (1974). We have recently published the results of a study (Inhelder *et al.*, 1975) which show stable acquisition of conservation notions as of age 5 if the following procedure is used: rather than merely deforming an object such as a ball of clay or modifying a collection of discrete elements, one removes part of or an element of the object(s) and moves it to another spot. In this case conservation appears earlier because the child understands two things he did not grasp during the simple deformations: firstly, that changes in shape are the result of displacements, and secondly, that in the course of these displacements what appears at the end is identical to what was removed at the start (this is what Piaget calls 'commutability'). We highlight this piece of work in order to show the much lesser importance of chronological age which can so easily be accelerated or delayed according to circumstances. The main point is the mode of construction which obeys constant laws and this characteristic is best exemplified by constructivism as we have defined it earlier.

We would also like to add that the recent discoveries of T. Bower and others concerning the innateness of certain behaviours which Piaget had not observed at the sensorimotor level do not contradict constructivism, since these primitive reactions do not directly result in higher-order behaviours but are reconstructed on different levels. These reconstructions are themselves not innate, but evidence of the constructive activities we have already observed elsewhere.

I should like to congratulate Dr Sohan and Celia Modgil on their fine effort in bringing together in these eight volumes the numerous pieces of work, thus rendering them accessible to researchers. We sincerely hope that this will encourage further progress in genetic psychology and all its applications.

Bärbel Inhelder,
University of Geneva

PREFACE

The eight volumes in the present series, *Piagetian Research*, together with the previous publication, *Piagetian Research: A Handbook of Recent Studies*, 1974, are intended to serve a wide range of needs for both teacher and learner at all levels: for university and college lecturers; post-graduate research students; those training to be educational psychologists; teachers and others following a wide range of advanced diploma courses; and education and psychology students at undergraduate level, following Educational and Developmental Psychology options. Research projects have been included which have implications for psychiatrists, paediatricians, rehabilitation and social workers.

In one sense, there are many authors to these volumes. The research evidence included is dependent on the countless efforts of Piaget's followers. In fairness, our gratitude is extended to those followers whose researches contribute immeasurably to the contents of these volumes. In particular, we acknowledge the cooperation of the many researchers personally communicating and forwarding papers for inclusion. Some collaborators have contributed material previously unpublished. These contributions, together with their accompanying correspondence, have resulted in a more comprehensive output.

We owe a very special debt of gratitude to Geneva University, and to universities here and abroad. Likewise, the inspiration of Professors Piaget and Inhelder, together with the general support of Professor Ruth Beard, Dr Gordon Cross, and Professor Marcel Goldschmid, are acknowledged.

It is an honour to have received such distinguished recognition for the volumes from Professor Bärbel Inhelder's gracious Foreword. We offer sincere thanks and gratitude for her interest and involvement and for the pleasant meeting in Geneva.

Enver Carim, an author in his own right as well as a perceptive editor, has provided the expertise necessary for such an ambitious series. Further to these more direct qualities Enver Carim has a profound philosophy with respect to a number of areas of knowledge including psychology and unusual drive and energy. We are indebted to him for all his support and acknowledge with gratitude the tremendous contributions he has made to this series.

Sohan Modgil
Celia Modgil
January 1976

INTRODUCTION

The eight volumes in the present series *Piagetian Research* together with the previous publication *Piagetian Research: A Handbook of Recent Studies*, 1974, are designed to make available a substantial number of Piaget-oriented researches that may be useful for immediate information as well as for long-term reference. The accelerating expansion of Piagetian research has led to an acute need for a source book more comprehensive than the ordinary textbook but more focused than the scattered periodical literature. More specifically, it should give the reader access to source materials that elaborate upon most Piagetian topics. Likewise, such volumes should offer students examples of a variety of approaches utilized by researchers in their efforts to investigate cognitive development. The numerous researches assembled present experimental subjects whose chronological ages range from birth to 98 years. The intended readership is therefore broad, from those interested in the very young, in adolescents, in the elderly.

The present volumes, as well as recording the replications and extensions of Piaget's work, include reflections on, speculations about, and analyses of the various problems of the theory. Hopefully, this should in turn provide inspiration for further elaboration, extension and revision. The research worker is provided with a broad spectrum of original sources from which an appreciation in depth of the theoretical, methodological and practical questions relevant to a Piagetian framework can be obtained. While it is conceded that a secondary source is not the ideal way to comprehend the theory, nevertheless it can provide the reader with a basic direction to the problem at hand.

The material gathered has been heavily drawn from University degree theses, published and unpublished researches up to and as recent as December 1975.* It became apparent that the subject matter was voluminous and that there were many ways to subdivide the Piagetian cognitive researches. In choosing the articles, the criteria were made as

---

* The authors have been alert to studies appearing up to January 1976 (after the completion of the main manuscript) and brief details of further selected researches have been added in order to enrich particular areas of inquiry and discussion. Hopefully, researches within this category will receive full treatment in anticipated follow-up volumes.

objective as possible, while recognizing that a personal slant is bound to influence the selection. Despite an extensive search it is not unlikely that valuable articles have been overlooked. To these researchers apologies are extended. In assembling these researches the principal objective was to include only those which satisfy one of the following criteria: Piaget-oriented (replications or extensions); developmental in nature; or those which have discussed their findings within the Piagetian framework.

The tables of content reflect a broad range of studies, and represent most of the major subdivisions of Piagetian literature. It must be pointed out that while some articles fall naturally into certain specific volumes, others would have fitted simultaneously into more than one volume, this being in part due to the inability to distinguish between the analytic and synthetic. Consequently, it was difficult to select one single scheme that would satisfy all readers and many arbitrary decisions had to be made. There is obviously considerable reliance on the use of cross references.

The compilation covers fifteen areas, assembled in eight volumes — each volume focuses on one/two major aspects of Piaget's work. The main areas covered are: Piaget's Cognitive Theory and his major works, Sensorimotor Intelligence, Conservation, Training Techniques, Logic, Space, Handicapped Children, Cross-Cultural Research, The School Curriculum, Morality, Socialization, Test Development, Animism, Imagery and Memory.

Each volume consists of an integrated review of the range of recent studies followed by abstracts of these researches arranged, in the main, alphabetically. Where details of early research are essential to illustrate the evolution of a particular area of study, these are not represented by a full abstract, but are included in the introductory review. Although many cross references to related abstracts are included, the reviews preceding the abstracts are not intended to be fully critical of the validity and reliability of experimental design. This is partly due to the fact that, unless full details are available (sometimes these have neither been published fully, nor the definition of concepts made meaningful), this would be inimical, and partly because the amount of work involved in a critical evaluation of every study in a work of this breadth would be prohibitive.

In comparison to most publications, an unusual amount of detail of researches is made available, and to accompany this with an equal amount of discussion, although essential, could introduce complexity in the aims of the volumes. Some of the abstracts (indicated by an asterisk) have been written by the authors themselves and reproduced in their entirety. It is realized that some abstracts are of only marginal importance, yet their inclusion is essential to show general developmental patterns.

It is the authors' intention that the reader, having investigated the range of available material, would then consult the original research according to his specific interests. Advanced research depends a great deal on what sources and data are available for study, and there is a consequent tendency for some parts of the field to be ploughed over and over again, while others remain virtually untouched.

The list of references included at the end of each volume together form a comprehensive bibliography encompassing over 3,500 references. Volume One additionally includes a comprehensive survey of Piaget's works, arranged chronologically.

Every care has been taken to report the results of the researches as accurately as possible — any misinterpretation of the results is accidental. It must be conceded that all the studies included do not receive equal coverage. While the overall response to the circulated requests was excellent, some shortcomings in the volumes are due partly to some failure of response. While deficiencies of the final product are our own responsibility, they exist in spite of a number of advisers who gave their time generously.

PART ONE

Jean Piaget:

a. An appreciation

b. Piaget's major works

a. An appreciation

It is probably natural to baulk at the task of paying tribute to a man of such stature. One's diffidence is further emphasized by the likelihood that an appreciation recorded now will be of limited value: the true import of Piaget's work will only be perceived in the fullness of time. The eight volumes in this series of *Piagetian Research* attest to the magnitude of Piaget's contribution to psychology and the very high esteem in which he is held. This appreciation will therefore limit itself to a recollection of Piaget's early life, an outline of his major works, together with a review of the present impact of his work. Again, it is necessary to focus on the constraints of such an undertaking, for within limited space, an outline will need to be selective and there is no pretence at offering a comprehensive treatment of Piaget's monumental work.

Some of Piaget's works are now regarded as classics in their field and many have been translated into numerous languages. His devotion and indefatigability in research have resulted in a current bibliography which has been estimated (Elkind, 1967, p. 164)[1] to amount to eighteen thousand printed pages (the equivalent of seventy-five two-hundred-fifty-page books!) and it is not yet complete! Thus the works published by Piaget and his associates during the past fifty years constitute the largest repository of knowledge about the cognitive development of children that is available anywhere.

Although it would not be inappropriate to describe Piaget as a biologist, philosopher, logician and psychologist, he himself prefers to be known as a genetic epistemologist, that is, one who attempts to get at the problem of the origin and development of knowledge. Piaget held Chairs in Philosophy at Neuchâtel, his home town, at the age of 29; in

---

[1] ELKIND, D., (1967) 'Biographical Note', Cited in PIAGET, J. *Six Psychological Studies*. New York: Random House.

Sociology and History of Scientific Thought at the Institut
Jean-Jacques Rousseau; in Genetic Psychology at the University of Paris
(Sorbonne); in Psychology and Science at Geneva where he retired in
1971 after 31 years. At the Geneva Centre for Genetic Epistemology
which Piaget founded in 1956, he continues to chair seminars attended
by logicians, mathematicians, biologists and psychologists which allows
him to further refine his work on the logical structure of knowledge
and its relation to the psychology of the child.

Born in 1896 of a historian father and an intelligent and religious
mother, Piaget[1] developed an early interest in biological sciences which
led to his first published paper at the age of eleven and an offer of the
post of curator of molluscs at the Geneva Natural History Museum
resulting from the publication of a series of articles on shellfish at the
age of fifteen. An introduction to philosophy, particularly the works of
Bergson and Kant, together with readings in religion and logic, led to an
involvement with the origin and nature of knowledge which Piaget felt
could not be satisfied solely by philosophy or by science and he
speculated about the linkage between the two.

After submitting his doctorate thesis on molluscs at the age of 21,
Piaget worked in psychological laboratories in Zurich and at Bleuler's
(the neurologist who once trained Freud) psychiatric clinic, followed
by two years at the Sorbonne involving studies in abnormal psychology,
logic, epistemology and the philosophy of science. Working with Simon
in the Binet Laboratory in Paris standardizing Burt's intelligence tests,
Piaget focused on children's incorrect answers and concluded that there
were qualitative differences in the answers of children of different ages,
causing him to refute a quantitative notion of intelligence. In this
context Piaget further developed the clinical technique originally learnt
from Bleuler and extended it together with the manipulation of various
concrete materials in his work with abnormal children at the Salpetrière
Hospital in Paris. His concomitant study of logic permitted him to
deduce the close relationship between thought and logic. These
intensive observations and revelations led Piaget to reconcile his various
intellectual commitments by accepting that psychological theory could
make use of biological concepts, intelligence being viewed in terms of
the organisms adaptation to its environment and further, that a full
understanding of human knowledge could be gained through the study

---

[1] Two of the several volumes in which Piaget has written short autobiographies
are: (i) PIAGET, J. (1952) 'Autobiography', in BORING, E.G. *et al.*, (Eds.)
History of Psychology in Autobiography. Volume IV, pp. 237—256: Worcester,
Mass.: Clark University Press; (ii) PIAGET, J. (1966) *Jean Piaget et les Sciences
Sociales*, Cahiers Vilfredo Pareto, No. 10, Geneva: Librairie Droz.

of its formation and evolution in childhood. Piaget therefore channelled his endeavours to the determination of these ends.

As a result of Piaget's early writings on child development, Claparède, the Director of the Jean-Jacques Rousseau Institute in Geneva, offered Piaget the post of Director of Research at the Institute which gave considerable impetus to his studies, leading to the publication of his first five books on children during the period 1923 to 1932. Describing naturalistic and experimental observations on the child's use of language (*Language and Thought in the Child*, 1923), the changes in certain types of reasoning from early to late childhood (*Judgment and Reasoning in the Child*, 1924), the mode in which the child views the world (*The Child's Conception of the World*, 1926), the child's ideas of natural phenomena (*The Child's Conception of Physical Causality*, 1927) together with the development of moral judgment (*The Moral Judgment of the Child*, 1932), Piaget regarded his efforts as tentative drafts and was surprised at the widespread attention they received. The questionable, entirely verbal technique was a shortcoming only later realized by Piaget when he recalled his use of manipulative materials with the abnormal children at Salpetrière Hospital. The second shortcoming, the lack of suitable constructs to describe logical operations, was also only later remedied. However, intellectual development proceeding through a series of stages and the differences between child and adult thought were clear features in even these early works.

The period 1920–30 witnessed the birth of his three children which consequently contributed to the publications of *The Origins of Intelligence in the Child* and *The Construction of Reality in the Child*, both published in 1936 forming a study of infancy, consisting of observations collected in collaboration with his wife, in which the origin of thought from action rather than language was clarified. This increased emphasis on action caused Piaget to remedy his temporary omission of manipulable materials in his testing procedures. During the next ten years Piaget received professional recognition through his appointment as Professor of the History of Scientific Thought at Geneva University and Co-Director of the Jean-Jacques Rousseau Institute and was prominent in its consequent amalgamation with the University of Geneva. His role in international affairs was established through the chairmanship of the International Bureau of Education later incorporated into UNESCO.

Piaget's developing emphasis on the importance of the child's activity in the formation of thought together with his concentration on scientific thought led to research collaborations with Bärbel Inhelder and Alina Szeminska: *Le Développement des Quantités Physiques Chez l'Enfant*, published with the assistance of Inhelder concerned the conservation of substance and weight and *The Child's Conception of Number*, co-authored with Szeminska. In 1942, Piaget published *Classes, Relations and Numbers*, a detailed account, formulated with the aid of logic, of the mental operations of the child from seven to eleven, termed 'concrete operations'. This was further elaborated in 1949 with *Traité de Logique*, expanding the logical model and formulating hypothesized structures present in adolescent cognition.

Piaget and his associates further focused on the perceptual research of the Gestalt psychologists. During the period of 18 years from 1943, a number of articles and reports were prepared resulting in the publication of *The Mechanism of Perception*, in 1961. Piaget holds that perception is an integral part of intelligence and that during the logic-like processes, the child's perception becomes progressively decentred and is gradually freed from its earlier domination by the field effects.

With some influence from Einstein, Piaget investigated the child's notions of time, velocity and movement, results of which were published in 1946 in *Le Développement de la Notion de Temps Chez l'Enfant*, and *The Child's Conception of Movement and Speed*. The same year saw the publication of *Play, Dreams and Imitation*, concerned with symbolic thought and relating back to his earlier observations of his own children.

Piaget continued his concerns with the Kantian concepts by following his earlier investigations of time, speed and number by further research, collaborated with Inhelder and Szeminska, into space and geometry published as *The Child's Conception of Space*, and *The Child's Conception of Geometry*, in 1948. Such a plethora of publications resulted in worldwide recognition and Piaget received honorary degrees from universities in various countries including America. An overview of his theory of mental development was contained in *The Psychology of Intelligence*, published in 1947.

The 1950s allowed Piaget to concentrate his efforts on his other major concerns — the problems of genetic epistemology. Initially in 1950, *Introduction à L'Epistémologie Génétique*, a three volume work dealt with the implications of his developmental findings for epistemological problems in mathematics, physics, biology, psychology and sociology. A grant from the Rockefeller Foundation in 1956 aided Piaget in establishing an International Centre for Genetic Epistemology within the Faculty of Science of Geneva University, allowing eminent scholars interested in epistemology to be invited to the Centre for collaboration with Genevan psychologists on issues relating to genetic epistemology. Over the years a series of volumes *Studies in Genetic Epistemology* have been published. Simultaneously Piaget further extended his logico-algebraic models of mental structures with the publication of *Essai sur Les Transformation des Operations Logiques*, 1952, particularly dealing with propositional logic. With the publication of *The Growth of Logical Thinking from Childhood to Adolescence* (Inhelder and Piaget, 1958), Piaget was able to present the most complete account of his stages in the development of logical thinking. From further developments to the symbolic model by Piaget and a systematic empirical study of the induction of physical laws in children and adolescents by Inhelder, a 'striking convergence' was found between the empirical and analytic results. Although having previously stressed a stage of development beginning at 11 to 12 years, Inhelder's data indicated a period of new structuring leading to another level of equilibrium at about 14 to 15 years. This set of operational structures were found to be based on propositional logic and a 'formal' mode of thought and further, the techniques of propositional logic were inadequate to analyze the integrated structures of operations. In attempting to explain the additional presence of a series of operational schemata, namely combinatorial operations, propositions, double-systems of reference, a schema of mechanical equilibrium (equality between action and reaction), multiplicative probabilities and correlations etc. together with propositional logic, Piaget found it necessary to refer to the 'integrated structures' on which they were based; that is, to the dual structure of the lattice and the group of four transformations. In 1959 *The Early Growth of Logic in the Child* was published utilizing logical models to describe the mental strategies of the child from seven to eleven years.

Behaviours and thought developments, the creation of logic, perception and emotion formed the core of *Six Psychological Studies*, in 1964. Philosophical and sociological notions were expounded in *Sagesse et Illusions de la Philosophie* and *Études Sociologiques* in 1965. The accelerating expansion of their publications led Piaget and Inhelder to recognize an acute need for a synthesis of their work and a definitive summary was presented in *The Psychology of the Child*, 1966. In the same year they also published a study of the development of imaginal representation: *Mental Imagery in the Child*, a study of types of imagery, their nature, their temporal and causal relationships with one another and with levels of cognitive functioning. Mental imagery is categorized into static imagery and anticipatory imagery: the former, when images are not capable of representing even the simplest movements or transformations, is characteristic of the pre-operational stage; the latter, dependent on operational thought, permitting flexibility and transformations in space. The next two years saw the publication of *Biologie et Connaissance*, and *Memoire et Intelligence*, respectively in 1967 and 1968. The former studied the relations between biological factors and the cognitive processes, while the latter concerned itself with the memory processes of the child, in relation to the development of intellectual functioning. Piaget's thinking on methodology is exemplified in *Structuralism*, 1968. The concept of structure comprises three ideas: those of wholeness, that of transformation and of self-regulation. Piaget, more recently, 1973, concerned himself with describing the trends in contemporary psychological science together with interdisciplinary progress and various applications of psychology in *Main Trends in Psychology*, originally published by UNESCO in 1970.

Therefore, as has been observed, great intellectual stature can be attributed to Jean Piaget. It can be speculated that his influence will pervade future research for many decades to come and occupy a most significant role in the history of the evolution of human understanding. His theory allows optimism and the possibility of continued growth in many spheres. Piaget's work has inspired replication, extension, speculation and revision. Piaget's theory is in full vigour; the research journals abound with further validation or extensions of Piaget's work, in a continuing search for further understanding of the issues raised. The numerous researches present experimental subjects whose chronological ages range from birth to 98 years, therefore being applicable to those interested in the very young, in adolescents, in the elderly. The plethora of studies relating to conservation acquisition in young children indicates its popularity in cognitive developmental research. This is due to the central role it has played in the research and theorizing of Piaget. The concept of object permanence, normally developed during the sensorimotor period, has been investigated and elaborated not only among infants but also animals. It has been the intent of many psychologists to accelerate certain Piagetian concepts via training techniques, although this trend has received little sympathy from Piaget himself who considers that it remains to be decided to what extent it is beneficial — 'one must ask whether the progress obtained is stable or whether, like many things learned in school, it disappears with time', 1974. The growth of spatial concepts and of logic in young children has received much attention although investigations into formal operational structures have only recently gained momentum due to an increasing focus upon adolescence in society. The investigations of Piagetian reasoning among intellectually handicapped children have provided further validation for Piaget's developmental sequence and interesting adjuncts have been obtained from researches among children impeded by visual and hearing impairments, together with those with brain dysfunction. Perhaps in no other area of psychology is there so much cross-cultural and cross-social-class empirical research data available as on the Piagetian tasks. Piaget's objective of studying the mental processes and thought structures underlying judgments concerning a variety of problematic moral situations has stimulated research into many associated factors namely cognitive, social, religious and cultural. Piaget's initial work has resulted in a considerably elaborated and refined moral developmental theory of Kohlberg which is gaining increasing attention. Early cognitive/psychoanalytic reconciliation attempts namely by Anthony and Wolff have only recently been extended through studies comparing the performance of emotionally disturbed children with normal children, together with research into the relation of personality and socialization factors to Piagetian concepts. Piaget has acknowledged his interest in these variables but he believes that in the psychology of child development there is so much to be learnt, so many unknowns that this would be the first work of a psychologist who is fortunate enough to be able to undertake experiments. Some recent research projects have engaged in the development of cognitive scales based on Piaget's theoretical formulations. Modgil's 1974 publication[1] *Piagetian Research: A Handbook of Recent Studies*, together with the present eight volumes in the series *Piagetian Research*, bear witness to the involvement and industry of hundreds of investigators anxious to elucidate this intriguing research into human development.

The multi-disciplinary nature of Piaget's work and his ability to integrate ideas from varied sources has resulted in his thought and work becoming relevant to many professions: psychology, sociology, psychiatry, paediatrics and education. Piaget has not however been directly concerned with the application of his theories and in connection with education for example, considers that it is difficult to deduce good pedagogy from psychology: psychology gives facts, pedagogy is the practical application of these facts and it is not for psychology to deduce or develop pedagogical methods, a research task to be undertaken by educators or teachers. Piaget however addressed himself to the problems of education as long ago as the 1930s, was active on a UNESCO Commission in the early 1950s and published a new work on the science of education *Science of Education and the Psychology of the Child*, in 1969, and recently in an article written for a series of studies prepared for the UNESCO, Piaget (1972) has revealed an interest in the school curriculum in which he advocates a complete revision of methods and aims in education. Despite Piaget's reluctance to become directly involved in pedagogy, his work has considerable significance for education and teaching and much of the momentum of his work has been increased by the interest shown by educators. More recently, Piaget (1973) in commenting on mathematical education

[1] MODGIL, S. (1974) *Piagetian Research: a Handbook of Recent Studies.* Slough: NFER.

discusses the necessary conjunction between the logico-mathematical structures of the teacher and those of the pupil at different levels of development.

This résumé of Piaget's life and work cannot by any means be considered complete, for Piaget himself has indicated every intention of continuing his research activities. In conversation with Barry Hill, 1972, recorded in the *Times Educational Supplement,* Piaget emphasizes '. . . I have got all these experiments in manuscripts here, all these files to work through. I work all day in psychology. I'm 75 and I have to finish what I have to say in psychology before going into what I don't know. Then there are ideas which I should have had 20 years ago, which make it necessary to revise a number of Chapters. In relation to the work to be done I really felt an adult at the age of 60'. When further questioned regarding the recognition of the discovery of the final structures of knowledge, Piaget replied, 'There are no final structures'.

b.Piaget's Major Works
(arranged, chronological order)

PIAGET, J. (1923) *The Language and Thought of the Child*. London: Routledge and Kegan Paul. Translated by M. Gabain. (First English Publication in 1926) 319pp.

PIAGET, J. (1924) *Judgment and Reasoning in the Child*. London: Routledge and Kegan Paul. Translated by M. Warden. (First English Publication in 1926) 204pp.

PIAGET, J. (1926) *The Child's Conception of the World*. London: Routledge and Kegan Paul. Translated by J. and A. Tomlinson. (First English Publication in 1929) 424pp.

PIAGET, J. (1927) *The Child's Conception of Physical Causality*. London: Routledge and Kegan Paul. Translated by M. Gabain. (First English Publication in 1930) 309pp.

PIAGET, J. (1932) *The Moral Judgment of the Child*. London: Routledge and Kegan Paul. Translated by M. Gabain. (First English Publication in 1932) 418pp.

PIAGET, J. (1936) *The Origin of Intelligence in the Child*. London: Routledge and Kegan Paul. Translated by M. Cook. (First English Publication in 1952) 425pp.

PIAGET, J. (1937) *The Construction of Reality in the Child*. London: Routledge and Kegan Paul. Translated by M. Cook. (First English Publication in 1955) 386pp. (Basic Books Inc., 1954)

PIAGET, J. (1941) *The Child's Conception of Number*. London: Routledge and Kegan Paul. Translated by C. Gattegno and F.M. Hodgson. (First English Publication 1952) 248pp.

PIAGET, J., AND INHELDER, B. (1941) *Le Developpement des Quantités chez l'Enfant*. Neûchatel and Paris: Delachaux and Niestle, 339pp. English translation by Arnold Pomerans, published Routledge and Kegan Paul, 1974.

PIAGET, J. (1946) *Play, Dreams and Imitation in Childhood*. London:

Heinemann, (1951) and Routledge and Kegan Paul (1967). Translated by C. Gattegno and F.M. Hodgson. 296pp.

PIAGET, J. (1946) *The Child's Conception of Time*. London: Routledge and Kegan Paul. Translated by A.J. Pomerans. (First English Publication in 1969) 298pp.

PIAGET, J. (1946) *The Child's Conception of Movement and Speed*. London: Routledge and Kegan Paul. Translated by G.E.T. Holloway and M.J. MacKenzie. (First English publication in 1970) 306pp.

PIAGET, J. (1947) *The Psychology of Intelligence*. London: Routledge and Kegan Paul. Translated by M. Piercey and D.E. Berlyne. (First English publication in 1950) 180pp.

PIAGET, J., and INHELDER, B. (1947) 'Diagnosis of Mental Operations and Theory of Intelligence', *Am. J. Mental Deficiency*, 5, 401—6.

PIAGET, J., and INHELDER, B. (1948) *The Child's Conception of Space*. London: Routledge and Kegan Paul. Translated by F.J. Langdon and E.A. Lunzer. (First English Publication in 1956) 490pp.

PIAGET, J., INHELDER, B., and SZEMINSKA, A. (1948) *The Child's Conception of Geometry*, London: Routledge and Kegan Paul. Translated by E.A. Lunzer. (First English Publication in 1960) 411pp.

PIAGET, J., BOSCHER, B. and CHATELET, A. (1949) *La Genèse du Nombre chez l'Enfant*. In: *Initiation au Calcul. Enfants de à 7 ans*. Cahiers de pedagogie moderne. Paris: Bourrelier, 5—28.

PIAGET, J. (1950) *The Psychology of Intelligence*. London: Routledge and Kegan Paul. (French Ed. 1947).

PIAGET, J. (1951) *The Right to Education in the Modern World*. In: *UNESCO, Freedom and Culture*. New York: Columbia University Press, 67—116.

PIAGET, J. (1951) *Play, Dreams and Imitation in Childhood*. London: Heinemann. (French Ed. 1946) (Routledge and Kegan Paul, 1967).

PIAGET, J. (1951) *The Child's Conception of the World*. London: Routledge and Kegan Paul. (French Ed. 1926).

PIAGET, J., and INHELDER, B. (1951) 'Die Psychologie der Fruhen Kindheit'. In: KATZ, D. *Handbuch der Psychologie*. Basle: Schwabe.

PIAGET, J., and INHELDER, B. (1951) *The Origin of the Idea of Chance in Children*. Presses Universitaire de France. Translated in English by L. Leake, P. Burrell and H. Fishbein, 1975. Published by Routledge and Kegan Paul.

PIAGET, J. (1952) *The Origin of Intelligence in the Child*. New York: International University Press. (French Ed. 1936) (Routledge and Kegan Paul, 1953).

PIAGET, J. (1953) *Logic and Psychology*. Manchester University Press,

48pp.

PIAGET, J. (1955) *The Construction of Reality in the Child*. London: Routledge and Kegan Paul. (French Ed. 1937).

PIAGET, J. (1955) 'Les structures Mathématiques et les Structures Opératoires de l'Intelligence'. In: PIAGET *et al.* (Publication Collective de la Commission Internationale pour l'étude et l'amélioration de l'Enseignement des Mathématiques). *L'Enseignement des Mathématiques*. Neûchatel and Paris: Delachaux and Niestle, 11—34.

PIAGET, J., and INHELDER, B. (1955) *The Growth of Logical Thinking from Childhood to Adolescence*. New York: Basic Books. Translated by A. Parsons and S. Milgram. (First English Publication in 1958). 356pp.

PIAGET, J., and INHELDER, B. (1956) *The Child's Conception of Space*. London: Routledge and Kegan Paul. (French Ed. 1948).

PIAGET, J. BETH, E.W., and MAYS, W. (1957) *Epistémologie Génétique et Recherche Psychologique*. (Vol. I des Etudes d'epistémologie génétique). Paris: Presses Universitaires de France.

PIAGET, J., and INHELDER, B. (1958) *The Growth of Logical Thinking from Childhood to Adolescence*. New York: Basic Books. (French Ed. 1955).

PIAGET, J. (1959) *The Language and Thought of the Child*. London: Routledge and Kegan Paul. (Paperback edition) 288pp. (French Ed. 1923).

PIAGET, J., and INHELDER, B. (1959) *The Early Growth of Logic in the Child*. London: Routledge and Kegan Paul. Translated by E.A. Lunzer and D. Papert. (First English Publication in 1964) 302pp.

PIAGET, J. *et al.* (1959) *Etudes d'Epistémologie Génétique*. Vols, 7, 8, 9, 10. Paris: Presses and Universitaires de France.

PIAGET, J. INHELDER, B., and SZEMINSKA, A. (1960) *The Child's Conception of Geometry*. New York, Basic Books. (French Ed. 1948).

PIAGET, J. (1961) *The Mechanisms of Perception*. London: Routledge and Kegan Paul. Translated by G.N. Seagrim. (First English Publication in 1969) 384pp.

PIAGET, J. (1961) 'The Genetic Approach to the Psychology of Thought', *J. Ed. Psych.*, 52, 277.

PIAGET, J., and BETH, E.W. (1961) *Mathematical Epistemology and Psychology*. Dordrecht, Holland: Reidel. Translated by W. Mays, 326pp.

PIAGET, J. (1962) 'The Stages of the Intellectual Development of the Child', *Bull. of the Menninger Clinic*, 26, 3, 120—8, Topeka, Kansas.

PIAGET, J. (1962) 'Will and Action', *Bull. of the Menninger Clinic*, 26, 3, 138—45. Topeka, Kansas.

PIAGET, J. (1962) 'The Relations of Affectivity to Intelligence in the Mental Development of the Child', *Bull. of the Menninger Clinic*, 26, 3, 129—37. Topeka, Kansas.

PIAGET, J. (1963) 'Explanation in Psychology and Psychophysiological Parallelism'. In: *Experimental Psychology: its Scope and Method*. Vol. 1, Chap 3, pp. 153—192. London: Routledge and Kegan Paul. Translated by J. Chambers.

PIAGET, J. (1963) 'Perception'. In *Experimental Psychology: its Scope and Method*. Vol. 6, Chap. 18, pp. 1—62. London: Routledge and Kegan Paul.

PIAGET, J. and INHELDER, B. (1963) 'Mental images'. In: *Experimental Psychology: its Scope and Method*. Vol. 7 'Intelligence', Chap. 23, pp. 85—143. London: Routledge and Kegan Paul. Transpated by Thérèse Surridge.

PIAGET, J. and INHELDER, B. (1963) 'Intellectual Operations and their Development'. In: *Experimental Psychology: its Scope and Method*. Vol. 7 ('Intelligence'), Chap. 23, pp. 85—205. London: Routledge and Kegan Paul. Translated by Thérèse Surridge.

PIAGET, J. (1964) 'Cognitive Development in Children', *J. Res. Sci. Teach.*, 2, 176—86.

PIAGET, J. and INHELDER, B. (1964) *The Early Growth of Logic in the Child*. London: Routledge and Kegan Paul. (French Ed. 1959).

PIAGET, J. (1964) *Judgement and Reasoning in the Child.* Patterson, NJ: Adams and Co. (French Edition, 1924).

PIAGET, J. (1964) 'Development and Learning'. In: RIPPLE, R.E. and ROCKCASTLE, V.N. (Eds.). *Piaget Rediscovered*. Ithaca: School of Education, Cornell University, 7—20, 176—86.

PIAGET, J. (1964) *Six Psychological Studies*. University of London Press. Translated by Anita Tenzer. (First English Publication in 1968.) 169pp.

PIAGET, J. (1965) *Sagesse et Illusions de la Philosophie*. Paris: Presses Universitaires de France.

PIAGET, J. (1966) 'Biology and Cognition', *Diogène*, 54, 3—26. Translated by Martin Faigel.

PIAGET, J. (1966) 'The Concept of Identity in the Course of Development', *Newsletter*, 8, 2—3.

PIAGET, J. (1966) 'How Children Form Mathematical Concepts', *Voprosy Psikhol*,. 4, 121—126.

PIAGET, J. (1966) 'La Psychologie, les Relations Interdisciplinaires et le Système des Sciences', *Bulletin de Psychologie*, 20, 5, 242—54.

PIAGET, J. (1966) 'Qu'est-ce que la Psychologie?'. Université de Genève, séance d'ouverture du semestre d'hiver. Geneva: Georg. 21—9.

PIAGET, J. (1966) 'Lettre à Romain Rolland, écrite en 1917. Action étidiante. (Genève). No. 69, p. 7.

PIAGET, J. (1966) 'Necessité et signification des recherches comparatives en psychologie génétique', *Journ International de Psychol.*, 1.

PIAGET, J. (1966) 'La Problème des Mécanismes communs dans les Sciences de l'Homme', Actes du 6e congrès mondial de sociologie, *Evian*, Vol. I, Association internationale de sociologie.

PIAGET, J. (1966) 'L'intériorisation des Schèmes d'action en Opérations Reversibles par l'intermédiaire des Régulations de Feedbacks. 18e congrès international de psychologie, Moscou, Symposium 24: 'Psychologie de la Formation du Concept et des Activités Mentales'.

PIAGET, J. (1966) Response to Brian Sutton-Smith, *Psych. Rev.*, 73, 111—12.

PIAGET, J. (1966) *La Situation des Sciences de l'homme dans le Système des Sciences*. UNESCO. Recherche international sur les tendances principales de la recherche dans les sciences de l'homme. 1ère version de l'étude, 1ère partie, Chap. 1, 15 avril, Polycopié.

PIAGET, J. (1966) 'Time perception in children'. In: FRAZER, J.P. (Ed.) *The Voices of Time*, 202—16. New York: Braziller. Translated by E. Kirky.

PIAGET, J. (1966) 'L'initiation aux mathématiques, les mathématiques modernes et la psychologie de l'enfant', *L'Enseignement Mathematique*, tome 12, fasc. 4, pp. 289—292.

PIAGET, J. (1966) 'Henri Pieron, 1881—1964', *Am. J. Psych.*, 79, 147—50.

PIAGET, J. (1966) 'Logique formelle et psychologie génétique'. In: FRAISSE, P., FAVERGE, J.M. and BRESSON, F. (Eds.). *Les Modèles Formels en Psychologie*. Paris: CNRS, 269—76.

PIAGET, J. (1966) *Autobiographie, Jean Piaget et les Sciences Sociales*. Cahiers Vilfredo Pareto. Geneve: Librairie Droz. 4, 10, 129—55.

PIAGET, J. (1966) *L'Epistémologie du Temps*. (Vol. 20 des *Etudes d'epistémologie génétique*). Paris: Presses universitaires de France. Chaps. I and 2. (Problèmes du temps et de la fonction', pp. 1—66 and (with the collaboration of M. Meylan-Backs) 'Comparisons et Opérations temporelles en Rélation avec la vitesse et la Fréquence', pp. 67—106.

PIAGET, J. (1966) 'Preface to ALMY, CHITTENDEN and MILLER *Young Children's Thinking. Studies of some aspects of Piaget's Theory*. New York: Teachers' College Press, Columbia University.

PIAGET, J. and INHELDER, B. (1966) *The Psychology of the Child*. New York: Basic Books, Inc. Translated by H. Weaver. (First English Publication in 1966) 173pp.

PIAGET, J. and INHELDER, B. (1966) *Mental Imagery in the Child*.

London: Routledge and Kegan Paul. Translated by P.A. Childon. (First English Publication in 1971) 396p.

PIAGET, J. (1967) 'Logique et connaissance scientifique', *Encyclopédie de la Pléiade.* Volume publié sous la direction de J. Piaget, Paris, Gallimard, 1345pp.

PIAGET, J. (1967) *Perception et Notion du Temps.* (Vol. 21 des *études d'epistémologie génétique*). Paris: Presses Universitaires de France – Introduction: p.1.

PIAGET, J. (1967) 'Psychologie et philosophie', Débat de J. Piaget avec P. Fraisse, Y. Galifret, F. Jeanson, P. Ricoeur, R. Zazzo, a propos de 'Sagesse et illusions de la philosophie', Raison Présente, (Paris, les editions rationalistes), No. 1. Expose: pp. 52–55, interventions: pp. 62–76.

PIAGET, J. (1967) 'Intélligence et adaptation biologique'. In: *Les Processus d'Adaptation.* Symposium de l'Association de Psychologie Scientifique de Langue Francaise, Marseille (1965) pp. 55–81. Paris: Universitaires de France.

PIAGET, J. (1967) 'L'explication en psychologie et la parallèlisme psycho-physiologique'. In: PIAGET, J. et FRAISSE, P. (Eds.) *Traité de Psychologie Experimentale.* Vol 1. ('Histoire et methode'), Chapitre 3. Adjonction a la deuxieme édition. Paris: Presses universitaires de France.

PIAGET, J. (1967) 'Cognitions and conservations: two views (a review of *Studies in Cognitive Growth*)', *Contemp. Psych.*, 12, 532–33.

PIAGET, J. (1967) 'Psychologie du psychologue', in 'l'homme à la découverte de Lui-même', encyclopédie *L'Aventure Humaine.* Vol. 5, Genève, Kister and Paris: La Grange Batelère.

PIAGET, J. (1967) 'Logique formelle et psychologie génétique', *Colloques internationaux du Centre National de La Recherche Scientifique.* 'Les modèles et la formalisation du comportement', Paris, 5–10 Juillet, 1965, pp. 269–276, Paris.

PIAGET, J. (1968) *Structuralism.* New York: Harper and Row. (First English Publication in 1971) 124pp.

PIAGET, J. (1968) *Epistémologie et Psychologie de la Fonction.* (Vol. 23 des études d'épistemoligie génétique, publiées sous la direction de J. Piaget.) Paris: Presses Universitaires de France, 238pp.

PIAGET, J. (1968) *Epistémologie et Psychologie de l'Identité*, (Vol. 24 des études d'épistemologie génétique, publiées sous la direction de J. Piaget). Paris: Universitaires de France, 209pp.

PIAGET, J. (1968) *On the Development of Memory and Identity.* Massachussetts: Clark University Press with Barre Publ. Translated by E. Duckworth 42pp.

PIAGET, J. (1968) 'Quantification, conservation and nativism. Quantitative evaluations of children aged two to three years are examined', *Science*, 162, 976–79.

PIAGET, J. (1968) 'Le structuralisme', Colloque de Genève: 'Structuralisme et symbolisme', *Cahiers Internationaux de Symbolisme*, 17–18, 73–85.

PIAGET, J. (1968) 'La genesi del numero nel bambino', *II Sedicesimo*, (La Nuova Italia, Firenze), 14–15, p. 15.

PIAGET, J. (1968) *Cybernetique et Epistémologie*, (Vol. 22 des études d'épistémologie génétique, publiées sous la direction de J. Piaget). Paris: Presses Universitaires de France. Forward, pp. 1–3.

PIAGET, J. (1968) *Six Psychological Studies*. London: University of London Press (French Ed. 1964).

PIAGET, J., and FRAISSE, P. (Ed.), (1968) *Experimental Psychology: its Scope and Method*. London: Routledge and Kegan Paul. (Seven volumes available in English translation).

PIAGET, J., INHELDER, B., SINCLAIR de ZWART, (1968) *Mémoire et Intelligence*. Paris: Presses Universitaires de France. (English translation, 1973). 487pp.

PIAGET, J. (1969) *Psychologie et Pédagogie*. Paris: Denoel (Bibliotheque 'Mediations'). (English publication to be published by Grossman-Orion Press, New York.)

PIAGET, J. (1969) *Science of Education and the Psychology of the Child*. New York: Grossman. Translated by D. Coltman. (First English Publication in 1970) 186pp.

PIAGET, J. (1969) 'Genetic epistemology', *Columbia Forum*, 12, 3, pp. 5–11.

PIAGET, J. (1969) *The Theory of Stages in Cognitive Development*. California Test Bureau Invitational Conference on 'Ordinal Scales of Cognitive Development'. Monterey, Cal., Feb 9, 1969. Maidenhead: McGraw-Hill, Translated by S. Opper. Now published in: GREEN, D.R., FORD, M.P., and FLAMER, G.B. (Eds.) *Measurement and Piaget*. New York: McGraw-Hill, 1971.

PIAGET, J. (1969) 'Quelques remarques sur les insuffisances de l'empirisme'. *Studia Philosophica*, Annuaire de la société suisse de philosophie, 28, 119–28.

PIAGET, J. (1969) 'L'epistémologie génétique', In KLIBANSKY, R. (Ed.) *La Philosophie contemporaine*, *Chroniques*. Firenze: La Nuova Italia. 243–57.

PIAGET, J. (1969) *The Mechanisms of Perception*. London: Routledge and Kegan Paul. (French Ed. 1961).

PIAGET, J. (1969) Foreword to FURTH, H.G., *Piaget and Knowledge – Theoretical Foundations*. Engelwood Cliffs, NJ: Prentice Hall, Inc.

PIAGET, J. and INHELDER, B. (1969) 'The Gaps in Empiricism'. In: KOESTLER, A. and SMYTHIES (Eds.), *Beyond Reductionism*. London: MacMillan, 118–48.

PIAGET, J., and INHELDER, B. (1969) *The Psychology of the Child*. New York: Basic Books Inc. (French Ed. 1966).

PIAGET, J. (1970) *The Child's Conception of Movement and Speed*. London: Routledge and Kegan Paul. (French Ed. 1946).

PIAGET, J. (1970) 'Piaget's Theory'. In: MUSSEN, P.H. (Eds.) *Manual of Child Psychology*. New York: Wiley, pp. 703—33.

PIAGET, J. (1970) *Science of Education and the Psychology of the Child*. New York: Grossman (French Ed. 1969).

PIAGET, J. (1971) *Structuralism*. New York: Harper and Row. (French Ed. 1968).

PIAGET, J., and INHELDER, B. (1971) *Mental Imagery in the Child*. London: Routledge and Kegan Paul. (French Ed. 1966).

PIAGET, J. (1972) 'A structural foundation for tomorrow's education', *Prospects*, Quarterly Review of Education, UNESCO, II 1, 12—27.

PIAGET, J. (1972) 'Piaget now', Parts 1, 2, and 3. (Piaget in discussion with B. Hill), *Times Ed. Supp.*, 11 Feb., 18 Feb., and 25 Feb., pp. 19, 19, 21, respectively.

PIAGET, J. (1972) 'Intélligence et mémoire', *Symposium de L'Association de Psychologie Scientifique de langue francaise, 'La mémoire'*. Geneve. Paris: Presses Universitaires de France.

PIAGET, J. (1972) *L'Epistémologie Génétique*. Paris: Presses Universitaires de France, collection 'Que sais-je?'.

PIAGET, J. (1973) 'Comments on mathematical education'. In: HOWSON, A.G. (Ed.) *Developments in Mathematical Education*. Proceedings of the Second International Congress on Mathematical Education. London: Cambridge Univ. Press.

PIAGET, J. (1973) *Main Trends in Psychology*. London: George Allen and Unwin Ltd., pp. 67. (Originally published as Chapter 3 in *Main Trends of Research in the Social and Human Sciences*, Part 1. Mouton/Unesco, 1970.

PIAGET, J. (1974) 'Foreword'. In: INHELDER, B., SINCLAIR, H. and BOVET, M., *Learning and the Development of Cognition*. London: Routledge and Kegan Paul Ltd.

PIAGET, J. (1974) *The Child and Reality*. London: Muller.

PIAGET, J. (1974) 'The Future of Developmental Child Psychology', *Journ. Youth and Adoles.*, 3, 87—93.

PIAGET, J., and INHELDER, B. (1975) *The Origin of the Idea of Chance in Children*. London: Routledge and Kegan Paul. Translated L. Leake, P. Burrel and H. Fishbein. (French Ed. 1951).

PIAGET, J. (1976) *The Grasp of Consciousness: Action and Concept in the Young Child*. London: Routledge and Kegan Paul, pp. 352.

PART TWO

Theory of cognitive development

a. Introduction

b. Sensorimotor stage

c. Pre-operational stage

d. Stage of concrete operations

e. Stage of formal operations

f. General criticisms

g. Interpretation and extensions

h. Applications to education

a. Introduction

As a developmentalist interested in the organism's adaptation to the environment through intelligence, Piaget, in the course of more than 50 years of concentrated research on mental development, has evolved a theory of intelligence. He established a sequence of age-related stages, from the early sensorimotor coordinations of infants to the abstract intelligence of adults. The stages are assumed to reflect maturational changes in forms of thinking, and the gradual acquisition of concepts reflects the influence of the physical and social environment.

Piaget states, 'I would ... define intelligence not by a static criterion, as in previous definitions [here he was referring to Claparède and Karl Bühler] but by the direction that intelligence follows in its evolution, and then I would define intelligence as a form of equilibration ... toward which all cognitive functions lead ... equilibration is not an exact and automatic balance, as it would be in Gestalt theory; I define equilibration principally as a compensation for an external disturbance' (1961). He goes on to argue that the compensation implies the fundamental idea of reversibility, and this reversibility is precisely what characterizes the operations of intelligence. An operation is always subordinated to other operations, is an internalized action, but is also a reversible action. Thus, Piaget defines intelligence in terms of operations and the coordination of operations.

He describes cognitive development in terms of stages, the criteria of which can best be defined in Inhelder's terms:

1. 'Each stage involves a period of formation (genesis) and a period of attainment. Attainment is characterized by the progressive organization of a composite structure of mental operations.

2. Each structure constitutes at the same time the attainment of one stage and the starting point of the next stage, of a new evolutionary process.

3. The order of succession of the stages is constant. Ages of attainment can vary within certain limits as a function of factor of motivation, exercise, cultural milieu and so forth.

4. The transition from an earlier to a later stage follows a law of implication analogous to the process of integration, preceding structures becoming a part of later structures.' (1962)

Piaget distinguishes four stages in the development of intelligence: first, the sensorimotor period before the appearance of language; second, from about two to seven years of age, the pre-operational period which precedes real operations; third, the period from seven to 12 years of age, a period of concrete operations; and finally, after 12 years of age, the period of formal or 'propositional' operations.

Piaget (in Mussen, 1970, p. 703) wrote '[it] is impossible to understand [my theory] if one does not begin by analyzing in detail the biological presuppositions from which it stems and the epistemological consequences in which it ends'.

b. Sensorimotor stage

Piaget captures the essence of the sensorimotor period when he says that a 'Copernican revolution' occurs in the child's cognition. Children in the sensorimotor period demonstrate a certain number of stages, which range from simple reflexes to the coordination of means and goals. Sensorimotor intelligence lays its premise mainly on actions, movements and perceptions without language. However, these actions are coordinated, in a relatively stable way, under what Piaget calls 'schemata of action'. This sensorimotor system is made up of displacements which, although they are not reversible in the mathematical sense, are nonetheless amenable to inversion ('renversables'). The child can return to his starting point and attain the same goal by different routes. In the coordination of these movements into a system, the child comes to realize that objects have permanence whatever their displacements.

Briefly then, the sensorimotor stage (approximately birth to two years) is characterized by development from a state of reflex activity to an organized sensorimotor action system which permits increasing mastery of objects in the environment.

Related studies include Decarie (1965) who constructed an object permanence scale, and whose findings lend further credence to Piaget's conclusions. Uzgiris and Hunt (1966) devised ordinal scales of the infant's psychological development (IPDS), which are receiving increasing attention. (See also Uzgiris, 1973). Roberts and Black (1972) employed the scales while investigating the effect of naming and object permanence on toy preferences. Wachs (1970) concluded '. . . its potential [i.e. that of the IPDS] for applicability . . . must be considered favourable.'

It is encouraging to note that the development of sensorimotor intelligence is receiving increased cross-cultural attention. The IPDS is currently being administered in Teheran and Israel (Dasen in personal communication with McV. Hunt, 1972). A study of object construction and imitation under differing conditions of rearing in Athens (Paraskevopoulos and Hunt, 1971) demonstrates high intercorrelations between levels of development in object permanence, vocal imitation and gestural imitation.

More recently, Woodward (1972) analysed the problem-solving strategies utilized by normal and severely subnormal children in tasks demanding rapid reasoning. Chronologically, the subjects were in the period between the end of Piaget's sensorimotor stage and the beginning of the intuitive.

c. Pre-operational stage

The pre-operational stage (approximately two to seven years) has received less attention than the sensorimotor stage. It is a transition period from the predominantly autistic and egocentric stage of early childhood to the early forms of social behaviour, sociocentric speech, and conceptual thought, which become more obvious toward the end of the pre-operational stage. Many of the problems which the infant faces at the sensorimotor stage reappear, since the child in the pre-operational stage must learn to adapt to the thoughts of others and to conceptualize his own experiences on a higher level of development.

The primary achievement of the pre-operational period is the emergence of what Piaget calls the semiotic function. Semiotic refers to the general phenomenon of signification — the business of making one thing stand for, or signify, another. In Piagetian terms, the first of these two things is a signifier, the second a significate. The key development in this period is the child's ability to differentiate between signifiers and significates, to recognize and use signifiers with the understanding that they are not identical with their significates. Piaget and Inhelder consider that at least five of these 'representative' behaviour patterns can be distinguished, the appearance of which are almost simultaneous and which can be listed in the order of complexity. The five patterns to which they refer are deferred imitation, symbolic play, the drawing of a graphic image, the 'mental image' and verbal evocation. Therefore this period is characterized by symbolic activity. The child develops symbolization and acquires more facility in language. During the pre-operational stage the child does not use logical operations in his thinking. Instead, he is perceptually oriented, makes judgements in terms of how things appear, and generally can deal with only one variable at a time. Thinking at this level of functioning is rigid. Thus, the pre-operational child cannot proceed from the 'particular' to the 'general' (induction), nor from the 'general' to the 'particular' (deduction). Instead, he proceeds from one particular to another. The notions he uses fluctuate incessantly between the two extremes of generality and individuality. Whereas the younger infant was self-centred in respect of sensorimotor actions, the pre-operational child is self-centred (egocentric) with respect to thoughts.

The stage can be divided into two further stages, namely the pre-conceptual stage (two to four years) and the stage of intuitive thinking (four to seven years). At the pre-conceptual stage the child operates on the principle of transduction: he is closely tied to the perceptual aspects of individual situations, and he is unable to form concepts. He has some general ideas, which Piaget calls 'preconcepts', i.e. a way of thinking midway between reference to specific objects and a genuine understanding of classes. Piaget believes that the development of mental imagery plays an important role in enabling children to anticipate recurring events and to plan actions in advance.

The second, more advanced phase (four to seven years) of the pre-operational stage is that of intuitive thought or intuitive use of concepts. The differentiation from the previous phase is a refined one. The judgement of the child at this stage is intuitive and subjective but deals with somewhat more complex configurations than in the previous stage. Piaget (1950) maintains, 'Intuition, at first dominated by the immediate relations between the phenomenon and the subject's viewpoint, evolves towards decentralization. Each distortion, when carried to an extreme, involves the re-emergence of the relations previously ignored. Each relation established favours the possibility of a reversal . . . Every decentralization of an intuition thus takes the form of a regulation, which is a move towards reversibility, transitive combinativity and associativity, and thus, in short, to conservation through the co-ordination of different viewpoints . . . which progress towards reversible mobility and pave the way for the operation' (pp. 138–9).

d.Stage of concrete operations

Around seven years of age, the construction of operational structures gives the child the means to know the world within systems of logical classification, seriation, numbers, spatial and temporal coordinates and causality. These systems and operations include such acts as those of compensation, identity and reversibility, all characteristic of children demonstrating full operativity. However, these operations do not deal with propositions or hypotheses, which appear only in the last stage of formal operations.

An illustration of these concrete operations is that concerned with classifying objects according to their similarity and their difference. This is accomplished by including the subclasses within larger and more general classes, a process that implies inclusion and is only fully operational around CA seven to eight years.

Therefore, during this period of development one can follow the genesis of thought processes. Nevertheless, it is still a long time before these structures can be applied with full operativity to all possible concrete contents. For example, the principle of invariance (constancy, conservation) is applied to the quantity of matter earlier than to weight, and to volume still later.

Briefly, during the stage of concrete operations (approximately seven to eleven years) mobile and systematic thought organizes and classifies information. Thought is no longer centred on a particular state of an object. It can follow successive changes through various types of detours and reversals, but because the operations are tied to action they are concrete rather than abstract. The attainment of the act of reversibility is the main feature in the development of the child's transition from pre-operational to concrete-operational thought.

Bruner (1959) comments 'in a general sense, by concrete operations we mean actions which are not only internalized, but are also integrated with other actions to form general reversible systems'.

The importance of conservation is well illustrated by Lunzer (1968) when he outlines the work of Piaget and others on conservation and observes: 'The importance of these experiments derives largely from the fact that they appear to bear out the appearance of invariants, which can serve as elements in the logical conceptualization of the world in terms of its quantifiable, spatial and physical properties'.

It should be mentioned here that alongside conservation there appears what Lunzer terms: '. . . a facility in applying certain logical relations both to objects and to these invariant properties. These logical relations are said to constitute well defined "structures" involving the operations of classification and seriation.'

Piaget (1953) argues that the period of concrete operations see eight 'groupements' of classes and relations, each of equal value in the study of behaviour at this period:

(i) Hierarchical classification: Most children (CA 8/9 years) learn to comprehend the relationship of a whole with its parts. However, some children of eight years could not believe that a member of the class 'Genevans' could also be a member of the class 'Swiss', for to them an individual could not belong to two classes.

(ii) Seriation or Order of Succession: Ranking an order of succession is based on appreciation of differences, whereas, in classifying, similarities are observed as well as differences.

(iii) Substitution or Equivalence: Children learn to recognize such relations as $14 = 13 + 1 = 8 + 6 = 5 + 9$ in number work, demonstrating varied ways of achieving the same outcome. Other alternative subdivisions of classes are learnt.

(iv) Symmetry: The understanding of reciprocity is typical of symmetrical relations. Children aged six appreciate that a distance is unaltered in whichever direction it is measured. At about eight years, most children comprehend that with two brothers each is a brother to the other.

(v) Multiplication of classes: When a child organizes objects into subclasses by considering concurrently shape and colour he will arrive at four subclasses which can be described in terms of both systems at once. Children, by approximately nine years, succeed in making complex multiplications of classes.

(vi) Multiplication of series: A multiplication of series is employed when a square in a map is spotted by both a number and a letter.

(vii) One-to-many equivalence in classes: When, for example, shapes are classified into triangles, conic sections, and quadrilaterals, with their subclasses, a 'family tree' of classes is produced. All of the subclasses circle, ellipse, parabola, hyperbola belong to the embracing class of conic sections.

(viii) One-to-many equivalence in series: Piaget has postulated five laws which the operations obey and reversibility is the most important.

Peel (1960) following Piaget's *Traité de Logique* illuminates further the nature of operational thought when he gives an outline of the logic of classes and differences together with the logic of the substitution of equivalent or symmetrically related elements. It is, of course, Piaget's thesis that there is a parallel between logical structure and mental structure which is operational. The case is strongly presented by Piaget (1950, 1952, 1953, 1964). A large number of cross-cultural studies within the framework of the concrete operational stage have been carried out. These are described in Modgil, 1974, pp. 226–257. Some of these studies have produced evidence that some subjects, even in the higher age group (12 to 18) do not reach the concrete operational stage. Dasen (1972) maintains '. . . it may be considered surprising, and a limitation of the universality of Piaget's stages, to find more and more evidence accumulating to show that concrete operational thought is not necessarily attained'.

e. Stage of formal operations

The last stage of intellectual development begins, on average, at 11 or 12 years of age and is characterized by the development of formal, abstract thought operations. The child becomes capable of reasoning, not only on the basis of objects, but also on the basis of hypotheses and is able to perform 'operations on operations', in a systematic manner. The formation of hypotheses and of deducing possible consequences from them, leads to a 'hypothetico-deductive' level of thought which expresses itself in linguistic formulations of propositions and logical constructions.

Combinatorial logic and proportionality are examples of formal thinking. In the experiment on combinatorial logic, the child is presented with five bottles of colourless liquid. The first, third and fifth bottles, combined together, will produce a brownish colour; the fourth contains a colour-reducing solution, and the second bottle is neutral. The child's problem is to find out how to produce a coloured solution.

In experiments on proportionality, the adolescent is given a candle, a projection screen and a series of rings of different diameters; each ring is on a stick which can be stuck into a board with evenly spaced holes. The instructions are to place all the rings between the candle and the screen in such a way that they will produce a single 'unbroken shadow' on the screen — the shadow of a 'ring'.

Briefly, it is around CA 12 that the child begins to comprehend in mathematics the knowledge of propositions, and becomes capable of reasoning by using different systems of reference simultaneously. The system remains flexible and can be elaborated indefinitely.

'The four principal stages of the development of intelligence of the child progress from one stage to the other by the construction of new operational structures, and these structures constitute the fundamental instrument of the intelligence of the adult' (Piaget, 1961).

Lovell (1968) maintains that a proportion of adolescents either do not reach formal operational thought at all or attain it in limited areas or for short periods. He cites the work of Hughes (1965) which involved a four-year longitudinal study of pupils, and stresses the slow cognitive advance among ordinary and even abler secondary modern school pupils; similar findings have been reported by Tomlinson–Keasey (1972), Stephens *et al.* (1972). A recent monograph by Peel (1971) draws attention to the few systematic investigations into the growth of thinking during adolescence, and describes a number of verbal situations which he, together with his students, has constructed for assessing the conditions under which adolescents make judgements. More recently, Kimball (1973) in testing 600 children and adults in Malawi (Central Africa), 80 in Mexico, 1200 in Uganda (East Africa) and several hundred in California, found very little (in some populations none) evidence of formal thought being expressed. Kimball (1975) in testing over 1000 'low achieving' students in seventh and ninth grades found 'most to be pre-concrete or concrete thinkers. Very few exhibit concrete–formal or formal reasoning, perhaps 5 per cent.' While investigating the performance of prospective elementary school teachers, mathematics student teachers, and honours calculus students on certain Piagetian tasks of formal operations, Juraschek (1975) found fifty-two per cent of the first group, one subject in the second group and none in the third group were at the concrete operational level. Five per cent of the first group were at the highest stage of formal operations, while 47 per cent of the second group and 64 per cent of the third group were at this stage. (The study is described more appropriately in Volume Three). The percentages of formal operational students enrolled in physical sciences classes at Guam University, among science 'majors' were found to range from 75.0 to 88.9 per cent depending upon cultural background (Waite, 1975). The percentage of formal operational students among 'non-science majors' was found to range from 27.9 to 45.7 per cent, depending upon cultural background. (The study is more appropriately described in Volume 3). Nolen (1975) indicated that one-half of the college students (N = 20) had not reached the stage of formal operations. (The study is more appropriately described in Volume Three).

A few cross-cultural studies have been conducted on formal thought – Goodnow (1962), Peluffo (1967), Were (1968) and Kelly (1970). These are discussed in Modgil, 1974 (pp. 226–57.) Such research evidence lends credibility to Piaget's 'prediction' (1966, p. 13; 1968, pp. 97–99) that the reasoning of 'primitive' peoples would not develop beyond the stage of concrete operations.

Recently, however, Piaget (1972) has speculated that formal reasoning may be used selectively rather than all-pervasively. Piaget (1972) in a theoretical article, 'Intellectual Evolution from Adolescence to Adulthood',* maintains, 'Growing out of a child's developmental history, formal operations become established at about the age of 12 to 15 years. Reflected in his ability to reason hypothetically and independently on concrete states of affairs, these structures may be represented by reference to combinatorial systems and to four groups. The essence of the logic of cultured adults and the basis for elementary scientific thought are thereby provided. The rate at which a child progresses through the developmental succession may vary, especially from one culture to another. Different children also vary in terms of the areas of functioning to which they apply formal operations, according to their aptitudes and their professional specializations. Thus, although formal operations are logically independent of the reality content to which they are applied, it is best to test the young person in a field which is relevant to his career and interests', p. 1. (Details of the article are given later).

In a study entitled, 'Cognitive development in adulthood: a fifth stage?', Arlin (1975) maintained that recent research relating to the Piagetian stage of formal operations 'suggest that consistent, progressive changes in thought structures may extend beyond the level of formal operations. The present study systematically searches for new structures. It suggests a new stage to account for these structures and offers empirical evidence to support the hypothesized fifth stage. Two formal stages are defined operationally: the problem-solving stage (traditional Piagetian formal operations stage) and the problem-finding stage. The commonly accepted criteria for a stage model are applied to justify the two-stage hypothesis. Particular emphasis is placed on the sequencing criterion and on evidence that the problem-solving stage is the necessary but not sufficient condition for the problem-finding stage. The discussion centres on the theoretical and empirical importance of considering the two-stage hypothesis, and further research questions are suggested', p. 602. (Details appear in Volume Three in the present series, *Piagetian Research*.) (Volume Three contains a full discussion of the stage of formal operations.)

---

* The French version of the article was presented at Foneme, 3rd International Convention, Milan 1970, and published in the proceedings (Foneme, Institution for Studies and Research in Human Formation, 20135, Via Bergama, 21 Milan, Italy.

f. General criticisms

As early as 1930, Hazlitt and McCarthy criticized Piaget's 1920s work for its heavy reliance on the interpretation of verbal statements, and the tendency to 'project' the experimenter's ideas into these interpretations. Commenting on these views, Dodwell (1960, p. 191) maintains that the 1952 English translation of Piaget's *La Genèse du Nombre chez l'Enfant* (1941) '. . . is an improvement on Piaget's earlier studies in at least two respects. First, the theoretical background is much more precise, but at the same time more elaborate than his earlier themes of cognitive development, and secondly the empirical investigations are more objective, described in sufficient detail to be essentially repeatable . . . ' In the 1940s, Piaget began to revise his earlier linguistically-oriented approach by posing questions concerning concrete materials instead of imagining these objects merely on the basis of a verbal description.

With respect to sensorimotor development Uzgiris (1973) states: 'While Piaget has used the term "stage" to refer to the six levels of advance in sensorimotor development which he described, he has not spelled out the underlying structural organization for each stage in the manner in which he has discussed the organization of thought processes characteristic of later stages in cognitive development. It remains somewhat unclear how definite a structural organization is to be expected for each of the levels in sensorimotor development, and how encompassing this structural organization might be across various domains of intellectual functioning'.

Pufall, Shaw and Syrdal-Lasky (1973) draw attention to Piaget's concern for the refinement of his earlier themes and, focusing on the development of number conservation, they state, 'In his original volume on number, Piaget (1952) identifies three stages in the development of lasting equivalence, while in a subsequent article (Piaget, 1968) he identifies a fourth stage which precedes the other three' (see Volume Two). Likewise, Berzonsky (1971) underlines Piaget's constant redefinement and elaboration of his theoretical formulations with his description of Piaget and Inhelder's *The Growth of Logical Thinking in Childhood and Adolescence* (1958) as a 'pinnacle of sorts' reached from Piaget's 1926, 1928, 1929, 1930, 1932, 1950 and 1953 works. Focusing upon the transition in cognitive operations from adolescence to adulthood, Piaget (1972) has published a theoretical discussion. In this account Piaget appears to weaken his earlier interpretations by advocating more stress to individual and societal differences in speed of development, developmental diversification, and professional specialization. Kimball (1973) maintains: 'Formal operations is not merely abstraction (abstraction occurs in all stages of intellectual development but is utilized differently), it is not isolated speculative statements or generalizations (sometimes but wrongly called hypotheses), it is not propositional logic or probabilistic thinking, it is not multivariate analysis, it is not information gathering. Formal operations is a total process embodying all of the above (and more) in a dynamic, model-building system of logical analysis.'

Bart and Smith (1974) have asserted, 'Definitional precision notwithstanding, Piaget has constructed a developmental theory of cognitive structures. In his theory, Piaget (1972) designated three major qualitatively distinct periods of cognitive development: sensorimotor, concrete, and formal. The order of development of the periods is contended to be universally invariant, as is the order for the sequence of stages that constitutes the periods. The rule-systems underlying the structure at various periods have been defined with varying specificity. Inhelder and Piaget (1958) have formalized the period of formal operations. Isaacs (1950) commented on the incompleteness of Piagetian logic and suggested that Piagetian logic be extended to account for multivalent or modal logical operations. Parsons (1960) commented on the lack of precision of Piagetian logic and in fact questioned even the intent of Piagetian investigation of adolescent thought. Bart (1971) extended Piaget's model of formal operations to account for possible development of cognitive structures within that period. The concrete operational period formalized by Piaget also has deficiencies. One primary weakness is the fact that Piaget provided eight mathematical structures labelled groupings I—VIII to depict concrete operations and ignored structural representations that may capture the totality and integration of the period (Flavell, 1963). However, Apostel *et al.* (1962) have attended to the filiation of these concrete operational structures. Piaget (1971) mentions the existence of a logic proper to the sensorimotor period, but neither references nor defines the axioms proper to the logic' (p. 163).

'Empirical evidence from experimental research on thinking has supported neither an independent cross-task logical capability, nor an equivalence of task difficulty within any one logical operation. Yet Piagetian theory has been constructed otherwise. Discussions of formal operations have emphasized characteristic abilities to separate form from content in logical argument (Gorman, 1972), without mentioning that the abilities may be intellectually accessible, but not psychologically available. Reapproachment between theory and research separate from the theory has been neglected', Nolen (1975).

Wallace (1972) draws attention to the question of the existence of stages which, he considers, 'remains as baffling as ever'. He reflects that the cross-sectional studies carried out by Piaget and his followers can never illuminate the child's development in conceptualization and that a longitudinal approach would give more definite results. Wallace calls for greater flexibility in aims for research studies lying in 'the acceptance of the inevitability of inconsistencies and individual variations in subjects' responses and in a consequent adjustment in the criteria employed in identifying developmental stages . . . this approach entails rejection of the aim of assigning particular individuals to single stages characterizing their performance across all situations and based on hypothesized underlying structures with the constraints on the order of acquisition of inference patterns which this involves'. However, to balance Wallace's and other criticisms, attention needs to be drawn to Piaget's writings (1969) on the value of the developmental stages in education and science. So far as questions about natural phenomena are concerned Piaget comments, ' . . . such a development of response would seem to bear witness to a structural transformation of thought with age'. He acknowledges that the same results have not been observed everywhere and that inconsistencies must be recorded — however, if the reactions of younger children are compared with those of older, the existence of a maturing process has to be accepted. Nevertheless, Piaget comments that to posit, from this, the existence of inflexible stages characterized by invariable, chronological age limits and a permanent thought content, is to proceed to extremes. He states that characteristic ages are never more than average, that there are overlaps when passing from one test to another — ' . . . these overlaps . . . probably exclude the possibility of establishing generally applicable stage limits . . . ' — further, that 'each stage of development is characterized much less by a fixed thought content than by a certain power, a certain potential activity, capable of achieving such and such a result according to the environment in which the child lives'. Piaget continues that we can never obtain anything more from experiments than sorts of 'mental phenotypes' and that reactions are not absolute characteristics of a given stage. Nevertheless, it is apparent that common features can be determined and 'are in fact an index of the potential activity differentiating each stage from the other.'

Flavell (1972) offers 'some proposals' concerning the classification and explanation of developmental sequences of cognitive acquisitions. He discusses the constituents of a cognitive-developmental sequence and some of the methodological problems in the empirical validation and examines the difficulties of explaining an invariant or near-invariant cognitive-developmental sequence. He also argues that human cognitive development 'may exhibit significant asequential features in addition to the obvious sequential ones, and that a realistic, balanced view of such growth should take account of both sorts of features'.

'In their extensive review of Piaget's stage construct, Pinard and Laurendeau (1969) have concurred with the Genevans' assessment. On the other hand, Flavell (1970, 1971) and Flavell and Wohlwill (1969) have argued that there is no compelling reason why so much synchrony should be required. These latter writers base their contrary opinion more on the known empirical facts of cognitive development (facts which seem to indicate a preponderance of asynchrony) than on groupement theory *per se*. In a recent discussion of the generic concept of "stage", Brainerd (1973) has taken a third approach to the question. First, it was shown that, if the stage construct is to make any logical sense, then an organism possessing some specific defining attribute (called an "intensional trait") of a stage also must tend to possess the other defining attributes of that stage. Second, Piaget's developmental predictions were viewed in terms of this fact. Basically, it was shown that, if we take the constituent operations of the groupements as the defining attributes of a particular stage of mental development (as Piaget does), then the predictions of synchronous emergence of groupements within concept areas and synchronous emergence of operations within groupements are psychometrically inescapable. Brainerd concludes that either these predictions must be accepted as essential to groupement theory or we must admit that the theory cannot possibly be a legitimate model for a distinct level of cognitive functioning', Weinreb and Brainerd (1975, pp. 184 – 185).

More recently, Dudek and Dyer (1972) lent support for Piaget's notions of constant, irreversible succession of stage progression through an analysis of 65 children within the age range from five to nine years. The Ss were followed longitudinally over a four year period with tests of operational and causal thinking. 'By grade II (ages seven to eight) the majority of children had attained the terminal stage on all but two of the nine tests given. By grade III terminal stages had been achieved for all tests although progress was comparatively slowest on tests measuring causality. True regression was found in only 6.5 per cent of the total number of regressions which is less than 1 per cent of the total possible number of regressions. The highly regressing children were not less intelligent (WISC) than those who showed few or no regressions', p.

380. (Details of the study appear later).

A full discussion of the concept of stages can also be found in Mischel, T. (Ed.) (1971) *Cognitive Development and Epistemology*, pp. 25–60; and in *Cognitive Development in Children*, (1970) Society for Research in Child Development, pp. 55–73.

Flavell (1963), in a critique relating to Piaget outlines the various shortcoming of the latter's approach surrounding 'matters of theory and interpretation; matters of experimental design and data analysis and matters of the upward and downward relating of data to theory and interpretation'.

Whether or not the revised clinical method gives a reliable assessment of the child's abilities continues to be debatable. Some psychologists feel that the method is still too verbal (Braine, 1962) while others have demonstrated the reverse (Fleischmann, Gilmore and Ginsburg, 1966, pp. 353–68).

Piaget's questions to young children: an analysis of their structure and content was examined by Palfrey (1972). The author argues, 'The child's conception of the world cannot be deduced from his answers to questions. On the one hand his interpretation of the question may in itself reveal characteristics about the child's view of the world. The questions Piaget has put to children during his research, however, are either ambiguous or tendentious. Consequently, the answers received do not necessarily follow from the child's conception of the world but quite probably from his expectation of the kind of answer required', Palfrey (*ibid.*, p. 122). (Details of the study are given later).

Beilin (1971) argues, 'The Piagetian clinical interview is itself a source of some ambiguity, however, since it has not been carefully analyzed in relation to the character of the information conveyed to the child through the form of the questions asked, their order, the vocabulary content of the messages, the rule-ordered properties of the organization of inquiry as well as the organization represented in the materials themselves' (p. 114). Aebli (1963, 1970) has analyzed just this clinical procedure and has summarized the points mentioned by Beilin with the phrase of the 'prestructuring function of the problem posed by the experimenter,' (Aebli, 1963, p. 37). Steiner (1974) asserted, 'Geneva-type experiments therefore do not merely uncover structures, as the Genevans think they do. Cognitive structures are constructed ("elaborated", as Aebli puts it) *ad hoc*, even in the Geneva-type experiments. The acquisition of operational behaviour through diverse experimental techniques, however, seems to support — as Beilin remarks — the assumption "that the logical operational system is under the control of a genetic mechanism that only permits the programmed development of defined cognitive structures through interaction with the environmental inputs," (Beilin, 1971, p. 114). On the other hand, the child is able to construct conceptual systems (operations) through different techniques of interaction with the environment. The child's activity transcends the methodologies of the investigating psychologists. This is not to say that there are no differences of efficacy among the diverse techniques relating to the construction of operations. What we essentially need is a multimedia model or feedback system (e.g. Miller, Galanter, and Pribram's TOTE-model functioning in a multimedia manner). "Multimedia" may be understood in Bruner's sense, although his categories of representation seem somewhat too broad . . .,' pp. 895—896.

Wallace (1972) states '. . . he (Piaget) appears to have failed to resist the supreme temptation of capitalizing on the ambiguity of verbal response to derive support for his preconception . . . although verbatim protocols for a number of subjects are usually presented in his work on intellectual development, there is little indication that Piaget followed a systematic inductive strategy in moving from this data to the formulation of his theory of stages. On the contrary there is a case for viewing the children's verbalizations cited as simply illustrations of the appropriateness of a preconceived theory.'

In a study entitled, 'Is there an error of the standard?: A critique of Piaget's perceptual theory', Begelman and Steinfeld (1972) questioned on methodological and experimental grounds the concept of the error of the standard (e.s.), postulated by Piaget to account for systematic overestimates of the St. 'The e.s. has been invoked to explain apparent incongruities in data obtained from experiments on size-estimation, the horizontal—vertical illusion and the moon illusion. Piaget's interpretations of size-estimation data are criticized on several bases. These include: (a) a number of possible independent variables may be affected by the stimulus-reversal paradigm; (b) the lack of control over the activation of differential instructional sets seriously limits the validity of inferences concerning perceptual process; (c) judgmental baselines have been assumed, not empirically established. Data from control conditions, as well as those from two critical experiments utilizing the "retrieval" paradigm, continue to cast doubt on the existence of the e.s. in relation to a broader range of perceptual phenomena', p. 114.

Begelman and Steinfeld further argued that 'the methodological and experimental critique of one of Piaget's basic assumptions — namely, the operation of the error of the standard — raises serious questions as to the validity of his equilibrium models of perception. It is possible that the process postulated to account for both perceptual distortion, as in illusions, and perceptual conservation . . . is valid. If so, then Piaget must provide some basis other than the hypothetical e.s. to establish the credibility of his model. Further, the findings which cast doubt on the operation of the e.s., and hence his theory of perception, may have implications for his theory of advanced forms of cognition. In line with this, if there is little reason to believe in a basic assumption underlying Piaget's theory of perception, we may also question the equilibrium model which is put forth to account for the development of all aspects and levels of cognition. On the other hand, it may be that Piaget's perceptual theory is invalid, but that there is some validity for the process underlying more advanced cognitive operations. There is no doubt that Piaget's conceptualizations have been heuristic; whether they are valid is another, empirical question' (p. 113)

Boyle (1975) in a recent general criticism considered that Piaget is occasionally guilty of making misleading claims in respect of his work, because he characteristically appears to misunderstand the nature of his own contribution. Boyle emphasized that one of the major complaints of psychologists about Piaget is that he persistently ignores all psychological thinking other than the sterile behaviourism that is, in any case, a minor part of psychology. Piaget appears to consider that debate devoted to the role of the organism's activity and many other factors have been ignored by psychologists other than himself. He appears to believe that his own unique contribution is that of the objective establishment of the truth of the principle that the stress on activity is not new. Boyle quotes Piaget (1971, p. 141); 'The notions of the fundamental significance of childhood, of the phases of intellectual development . . . of true interest and activity, are already there in (Rousseau's) work, but they did not provide inspiration for the "new methods" until that moment when they were rediscovered, on the plane of objective observation and experiment, by authors more concerned with unfevered truth and systematic controls'. Boyle commented that he grants Piaget his concern with 'unfevered truth' but refutes his 'objective observation and experiment' with 'systematic controls'. He further criticized his general methodology (Boyle, 1975, p. 59). Boyle further elaborated that despite Piaget's claims he is not interested in reasoning individuals, but in what he calls the 'epistemic subject', i.e. what it is that characterizes all individuals at a given level of development. (Details follow.)

In counteraction an examination of the impact of Piaget and his theory on American developmental psychology, by Brumer (1975) involved asking six different groups of developmental psychologists to complete a questionnaire. Four cohort groups were defined by the year they received their PhD, a group of Piagetian researchers and a group of S-R researchers. The Piagetian researchers were noted to be a hybrid group, identifying with both the American and Piagetian definitions of development. They were, likewise, younger psychologists, many of whom had been introduced to the new ideas during their graduate years. Brumer obtained further confirmation of some of the changes in developmental psychology by undertaking a quantitative analysis of the growth of the field and by looking at quantitative and qualitative changes in the journal *Child Development*. 'These changes include a doubling of the literature every five to six years, an increase in the use of the experimental-manipulative approach, an increase in research based on theory and on Piagetian-related subjects, the predominance of studies on cognitive development and the secondary importance of socialization and affective variables.' (Details follow).

g. *Interpretations and extensions*

For Piaget (1970), development is considered as an epigenetic rather than a preformative process. Thus, Flavell (1963) and Hunt (1961, 1969), e.g., have gone to some length to argue for the differentiation and emergence of cognitive structures which are not reducible to previous structures (epigenesis). The view is that these structures gradually come about through an active organism interacting with its environment. Hunt (1961) presented substantial evidence against the doctrine of psychobiological preformation. 'The concept of increasing differentiation, together with hierarchical integration, is basic to organismic approaches to cognitive development. This developmental view is best summarized by Werner's (1957) orthogenetic principle, which states "there is a progression from a state of relative undifferentiation to a state of increasing differentiation and hierarchic integration" (Kaplan, 1967, pp. 82—83). As noted by Kagan and Kogan (1970), Werner actually meant by differentiation that there is a decrease in the interdependance both between parts within the person and between the subject and object rather than the idea that there is an increasing complexity or number of units. Piaget's theory of cognitive development appears to incorporate both of these meanings of differentiation insofar as cognitive structures become increasingly able to transcend the immediate situation and also increase in number and complexity' (Buss and Royce, 1975, p. 97).

Flavell's (1972) monograph offered some proposals concerning the classification and explanation of developmental sequences of cognitive acquisitions. He discusses the components of a cognitive-developmental sequence and some of the methodological problems that complicate its empirical validation. (Details appear later). Further, Flavell (1970) and Flavell and Wohlwill (1969) have proposed a classification of the general forms of change which might apply to the process of development. 'Since the classification provides for the addition and substitution of items of analysis (substantive discontinuities), the classification is, in this sense, more general than that proposed by Piaget. However, beyond this general comparison, there is little basis of similarity between Piaget and Flavell. Piaget is a deductive formalist; Flavell is an inductive empiricist. While Piaget's particular brand of formalism generates a too narrow perspective of the forms of admissible change, Flavell's eclecticism provides a set of categories linked to no explicit theory of structure. As Flavell summarizes, ". . . the categories finally arrived at have simply not proven to be the unitary, non-overlapping, definitionally-elegant affairs originally hoped for," (1972, p. 9)', Daele (1974, p. 3). Daele therefore in a paper entitled, 'Infrastructure and transition in developmental analysis', maintains that 'Psychological theories which provide a formal analogue to embryological development, such as Piaget's constructivism, deal with only a subset of the plausible forms of change. From Piaget's perspective, a structure is a system of transformations (Piaget, 1970a, 1971). The structure is "preserved or enriched" by the interplay of its transformations "which never go beyond its frontiers, nor employ elements that are external to it" (Wilden, 1973, p. 311). As Wilden argues, a Piagetian structure is therefore a closed structure, "a system closed under transformation", (Piaget, 1970b, p. 6). Even if it is admitted that the operations which organize structure in Piaget's sense are extremely general, and all that Piaget's constructivism argues is the necessity of a consistent application of rules of formation and regulation from stage to stage, the theory, nevertheless, excludes the substitution or replacement of structures. Stages follow one another in a state-determined way. Given the operation of the system invariants, the "stronger" structure necessarily follows from the "weaker" structure in a fixed sequence (Piaget, 1970b, p. 141). With Piaget, substantive discontinuity is inadmissible. But it is for precisely this reason that Piaget's constructivism deals with only a subset of forms of change because substantive discontinuity is plausible, and within a more general framework admissible', pp. 2–3.

Bart and Smith (1974) have contributed to the structural analysis of cognitive development by providing a precise formulation of the generic notion of cognitive structure. (Details appear later).

In a Paper entitled: 'Developmental and educational applications of Structure theory: a mathematical reformulation of Piaget's concept of structure', Dirlam (1975) stated, 'In Piagetian theory the concept of structure is one of the most significant (Piaget, 1970; Gardner, 1972) but it is also one of the most elusive concepts for research and educational purposes. Over the last five years several co-workers and I have developed a mathematical method for classifying and evaluating structures that can be readily applied to problems in cognitive and developmental psychology, semantic development, and the individualized evaluation of educational practices (Dirlam, 1972, 1973;

Dirlam, Courtney, Uttich and Hays, 1974a; Dirlam, Mendez, Michal, and Palm, 1974b; and Dirlam and Opitz, 1974c)'. (Full details are given later).

Langer (1975) formulates further propositions towards a 'comprehensive structural developmental theory of cognitive change,' begun in Langer (1969a, 1969b). The focus is upon: '(a) The organization of the subject's assimilatory operations and accomodatory figurations; (b) the intrinsic coordinations between the theoretical and empirical cognitions constructed, respectively, by these two kinds of functional structures; and (c) the cognitive developmental changes produced by intrinsic coordinations.' (Details follow).

Steiner (1974) was intent to focus the study on the question of the psychological reality of cognitive structures. An outline of Piaget's structural and Bruner's representational theories of cognitive development is presented, followed by an analysis of Piaget's concept of 'internalization', relating this to the concept of 'representation'. 'Cognitive structures are shown to be real exclusively in an actual representation. In that sense, this interpretation approaches a synthesis of Piaget's and Bruner's theories. To account for the construction of representation-bound structures (e.g. operations), microlevel processes taking place in a multimedial feedback system are to be focused'.

Piaget's work in early child development as it relates to Chomskian psycholinguistics was examined by Von Hippel (1972) who asserts that, 'Piaget claims that language differs from other symbolic activity by virtue of the representative medium involved and is similar to other symbolic activity by virtue of the cognitive structures into which this representative medium is integrated. The author agrees with the Chomskian view that this claim is unjustified. Piaget, like others who hold a similar position, does not present a sufficiently detailed description of the cognitive organization of different symbolic activities to justify the conclusion that they are similar. It is suggested that Piaget regards language primarily in its phonological aspect. This contrasts with the Chomskian emphasis on syntax. It is further suggested that Piaget's cognitive structures are the psychological counterparts to Chomsky's linguistic notion of a semantically interpreted syntactic marker . . . The nature of the intrinsic structure of the child at the onset of language acquisition is a principal area of disagreement between Chomskians and Piagetians'. (Details are given later).

A comparison was made between the developmental stages of Vygotsky and Piaget by Stewin and Martin (1974) in a study involving 104 subjects aged four through 16 years of average range of intelligence. The tasks administered were the Vygotsky Test of Concept Formation and the Piagetian tasks of the conservations of continuous and discontinuous quantity, weight, area, volume and density. Responses were scored qualitatively in terms of the described developmental model of each theorist. 'Developmental levels were converted to a numerical scale within each system and were compared through correlational analysis. The obtained results led to the conclusion that the two theoretical models are closely related in that both Piaget's and Vygotsky's models of cognitive development appeared representative of children's thought processes at all levels of sophistication'.

In an article entitled, 'Some comments on Fodor's "Reflections on L.S. Vygotsky's thought and language" ', Sinclair (1972) argued, 'In his discussion of Vygotsky's well-known work on language and thought, Fodor appears to equate Piaget's views on cognitive development with those of Vygotsky's. This is at least partly misleading. Though development in Piaget's theory is considered to proceed by stages, and though Piagetians indeed assume that "operations of a specific computational power are either available or absent across the board at any given developmental level" (under certain conditions, at least), they do not think of development as an accumulation of isolated new operations. Nor is it correct to imply that Piagetians, like Vygotsky, label certain concepts as "concrete" or "abstract". Piaget's stages are defined by system: systems of actions (during the sensorimotor period, before the infant becomes capable of representation), systems of one-way mappings or semi-logical functions (during the period of intuitive thought, until the age of about six), and systems of mental operations (at what has been called the "concrete" and "formal" levels of reasoning) . . . Inside the framework, there is no way to label the notion of "tableware" (to take one of Fodor's examples) as a sensorimotor, concrete or formal concept *per se* . . . The developmental view presented by Fodor has much in common with Piaget's theory. Piaget has always stressed the fact that babies exhibit a number of action-patterns, each of which formed a small organized totality, and that development consists in ever wider coordinations and integrations of such patterns . . . By contrast, when Fodor views development as a widening application of early installed . . . special purpose computational apparatus, thus assuming a difference in quantity rather than in quality at different developmental levels, this cannot be conciliated with Piaget's theory . . . The "ethological plausibility" of Piaget's developmental theory has been explored by Etienne (1972) and its biological basis has been formulated by Piaget himself (1967)', Sinclair (*ibid.*, pp. 317—318).

Cognition and the acquisition of selected function words in poverty children was studied by Hanes (1974). 'Based on cognitive-developmental theory and theories of language acquisition, an integrated theory of language acquisition was proposed. The major proposition of this integrated theory was that language acquisition is a result of an interaction between cognitive development and linguistic complexity. Cognitive development was discussed in terms of the developmental stages proposed by Piaget (1926). Linguistic complexity was broadly defined as the abstractness of the symbol in relation to actual perceptual events, as well as the number of transformational operations required in order to derive semantic content from a linguistic sequence', p. 4926 A. Hanes formulated hypotheses which considered the acquisition of selected function words, including three classes of subordinate connectives and the prepositional phrase in the reversible passive construction. Temporal, causal, and antithetical connectives were the three subordinate connective classes studied. The sample constituted black inner city, white rural, and bilingual Puerto Rican children, within the age range from six to eight years. A sentence repetition task consisting of 28 stimulus sentences was individually administered and all responses were tape recorded. Temporal connectives were acquired prior to causal and antithetical connectives and causals were acquired prior to antitheticals. That the differentiation of forms within a class does not occur simultaneously with the acquisition of a connective class was fully substantiated. (Details are given later).

To examine whether language development can be understood epigenetically in the same manner and based upon the same principles with which Piaget has analyzed intellectual-cognitive development generally, Moerk's (1975) study was subdivided into four parts: first, some basic principles in Piaget's system were discussed in their relation to language development. Next, the author analyzed how the functions underlying general cognitive development could also serve as tools for language development. The Piagetian concepts of structures or schemes were examined next, with respect to their relevance to linguistic structures. Finally, Moerk explored the preverbal development of several classes of contents or concepts and their early verbal equivalents. The author maintained that although Piaget has never explored language development in detail, the Geneva school contributed to developmental psycholinguistics in three important aspects: '(a) He has explored and formulated the functional principles which lead to cognitive acquisitions. (b) He has described the resulting structures as well as the effects these structures have upon further cognitive development. (c) . . . he has investigated some of the basic concepts and classes of concepts that are established during infancy', Moerk (*ibid.,* p. 166). Only the exploration of linguistic structures has been extensive and semantics has been discussed repeatedly (Chafe, 1970; Katz and Fodor, 1963; Ogden and Richards, 1923; Weinreich, 1963).

Further, the functions involved in language acquisition and language behaviour fall into the domain of the neurological and psychological sciences which have been neglected despite Peirce's (1932) and Morris'

(1946) emphasis on the pragmatic aspect of language. 'Only recently have meaning and functions come more to the attention of this new discipline. The cognitive-functional approach of Bever (1970), or Slobin (1973), the special consideration of meaning by Brown (1973), and the sociologically oriented analyses of Labov (1970) are examples of this . . .', (*ibid.*, p. 166).

Moerk concluded, 'Piaget, in his independent and innovative approach to the science of epistemology, has concentrated from the beginning upon these most primordial aspects, since only meaningful functioning can lead to complex structures and concepts. It will remain the task of the present generation of developmental psycholinguists to incorporate this fruitful and promising system more into their own scientific endeavours', p. 166.

Analogies between the acquisition of physical knowledge and the acquisition of language are suggested by Karmiloff-Smith and Inhelder (1975) from a series of experiments designed to study goal-oriented behaviour when reporting the 'action sequences' of 67 subjects between 4.6 and 9.5 years in a block balancing task. In an attempt 'to pave the way towards understanding the more general processes of cognitive behaviour, . . . the analysis focuses on the interplay between the child's action sequences and his implicit theories which the observer infers from the sequences rather than from his verbal comments. Emphasis is placed on the role of counter examples and on shifts in attention from goal to means. The construction and overgeneralization of "theories-in-action" appear to be dynamic and general processes which are not stage-linked.' (Details follow)

That predictions derived from dissonance theory should hold only for subjects who had reached at least the concrete operational level, but not for the pre-operational children was partly supported by Atwood's (1969) study where he found that only those children who had reached the concrete operational stage could adequately balance hypothetical triads as predicted from Heider's (1958) theory of balance — a theory similar to Festinger's dissonance theory. Blanchard and Price (1971) likewise, reported some relationships between Piaget's stages and preferences for balanced situations, although they found a puzzling similarity between pre-operational and formal operational subjects, both of which differed from the concrete operational ones. In continuation, Biaggio, Wegner, and Simpson (1973) hypothesized that children must have reached at least the concrete operational level according to Piaget's formulation in order to experience cognitive dissonance. No significant differences between pre-operational and concrete operational children in terms of dissonance predictions were computed. Experiment one showed significant sex differences 'in compliance with a prohibition, as well as interaction effects between sex and severity of threat, and between sex and probability of detection ... experiment three indicated that both preoperational and concrete operational subjects may experience dissonance', p. 175. The authors concluded by a discussion of the methodological difficulties involved in adapting dissonance experiments to children. (Details follow).

Riegel (1973) argued for an extension of Piaget's theory of cognitive development through a dialectic reinterpretation. He considered that development is interpreted as a continuing alienation from this basis culminating in the noncontradictory thinking of formal operations: which fail to represent adequately the thought and emotions of mature and creative persons. 'The ceaseless striving toward formal operations becomes inappropriate and ineffective for the level of dialectic maturity'. (Details are given later). Of further interest is Cassel's (1973, 1975) maintenance that a careful examination of the work of Piaget reveals that many of the very basic fundamentals exhibited by Maslow, credited largely with being the founding father of Humanistic Psychology, were even earlier embraced solidly by Piaget. Therefore, one may rightfully conclude from such empirical evidence that Piaget, like Maslow, is a Humanistic Psychologist. (Details appear later).

Information processing

Inhelder (1972) drew attention to the two kinds of knowledge in the Piagetian structural model. Knowledge of the properties of objects, from which are derived principles of operations (or logico-mathematical knowledge) not specific to the objects themselves. Piaget's work has concentrated largely on the logico-mathematical knowledge, paying little attention to knowledge of object properties. Inhelder maintained that the interaction of the two knowledge systems was vital for a comprehension of the developmental process. Inhelder, through a series of experiments on the conservation of number and length, suggested that Piaget had not really paid sufficient attention to object properties. Further, that a better understanding of the interaction between the two systems of knowledge could inform a process model seeking to explain the development of new structures. She suggested that conflict between the two types of knowledge is what could lead to the onset of a new structural level: 'It is this conflict which will trigger the process leading to the final resolution through reciprocal assimilation of the two sub-systems that do not necessarily belong to the same developmental level. The emergence of conflicts can explain the frequently occurring regressions in the subject's overt reasoning — they are only apparent regressions. In fact, they are observable symptoms of an internal event announcing the structuration of a higher order', Inhelder (*ibid.*, p.113). For Inhelder, then, concentration on the process as opposed to the structure which had been Piaget's primary concern, led to a reconsideration of the role of the structural elements, namely, representation and the interaction of the two kinds of knowledge. This new view of process was however always intended to be viewed within the existing Piagetian structural model: there was no suggestion that changes in the process model in any way affected the validity of the structural model. Walkerdine and Sinha (1975)* argued, 'Although Inhelder recognized the importance of "referential aspects of the situation" in terms of the properties of the objects which feature in the experimental situation, she made no mention of the social context which defines and transmits for the subject those perceptual properties of the objects which are determinant for the culture. Objects exist in a functionally and experientially defined framework (i.e. the context of the use to which the objects are put). Function is both socially and culturally defined. Apprehension of the properties of objects is not simply in terms of objects *qua* objects but of objects in socially defined situations. The apprehension of the properties of objects is focused in language. Language is both interpreted within social contexts but also helps to focus attention on particular aspects of the context at hand. This is exemplified by Donaldson *et al.*'s work . . . in which the interpretation of relational terms was seen as a highly complex process, since several possible interpretations of the terms existed and the individual had to know which interpretation best fitted the experimental context', p.20.

In an article: 'Information processing tendencies in recent experiments in cognitive learning — theoretical implications', Cellérier (1972) commented, 'Professor Frijda is reported (by Gascon, 1969) to have said, in an unpublished conference that "Piaget's theory is easier to programme than any other existing theory of intelligence". However, my impression is that Piaget's central concepts are not sufficiently specified in their present form to be programmable. His experiments are programmable, but their simulation should only be considered as a means to elucidating the nature of these constructive processes. This is what I wish to submit to a discussion here' (p. 115. Cellérier in his paper goes on to say that programming Piaget in the sense of simulating all Piaget-type situations would not be programming the essential Piaget, that is, the development of intelligence. He cites the experimental work of Gascon (1969a, b) and argued that Inhelder's (*op. cit.*) new line of experiments should partly elucidate the many problems still to be solved. Cellérier concluded, 'I believe structural and process models are not just theoretically complementary descriptions of the same

* Gratitude is expressed to the author, Dr Walkerdine, the editor, Dr Markova and the publishers, John Wiley & Sons Limited, for permission to include this quotation from *Language and the Social Context*, in press.

phenomena, but that they reflect — in a perhaps too stylized form — the constructive interplay of rules and concepts in actual thought. Children, or adults for that matter, use structural representations of their task environment to "compute out" on them possible courses of action. We call this process thought. It is not a random walk through a faceless maze, but more like the choice of a path through a somewhat uncharted one. Moreover, our rules of choice and the chart itself are constantly being updated by the discoveries we make not only on the maze, but also on our own methods of exploration. When we divest our representations of their contents, and our computations of their objects, we may, *a posteriori*, project thought on the two dimensions of structures and formal deduction systems. Further, I suspect the formative mechanisms Piaget defines, are not mere artifacts of the theory, but reflections of the processes that actually weave the two dimensions of our models into a functional performing system. I do not believe our representations are stored as permanently organized cognitive maps, but rather that we actively reconstruct the maps from sets of stored cues whenever we have a specific problem to solve in detail. When we do this, we integrate the relevant cues we may have accumulated since our last reconstruction. It is at this point that the final product — our cognitive maps — come closest to being models of the psychologist's structures. With practice, we may become better at the reconstruction of itself — that is, our rules for representation evolve. In this sense, structures are only *a posteriori* descriptions of the results of an evolving process. In the same manner, schemes should not be conceptualized as fixed, stored programmes or sub-routines, but as being reinvented more or less completely whenever they are called in on a specific problem. There again the final product may *a posteriori* be described as a formal system. In both cases, what we call development is the result of change in our reconstruction rules. How this change occurs is therefore the central problem in both structural and process theories. My conjecture is that it can only be solved by a synthetic approach describing a functional progressive re-equilibration that would somehow avoid infinite regressions into metarules and meta concepts by incorporating a cycle of alternating constructions of the meta-language of one category in the language of the other' (pp. 122—123).

h. Applications to education

The momentum of Piaget's work has been increased by the interest shown by educators — first and foremost by educators involved with young children (Susan Isaacs was much involved in correspondence with Piaget) but increasingly by those concerned with older children. Although the majority of replication and extension studies are carried out within the universities, the progressive involvement of teachers and college of education lecturers in advanced courses and research degrees implies a stimulation within the schools. When Piaget began his studies of genetic epistemology he was not concerned with educational problems and during the years has only occasionally commented on educational practices. Therefore, as with many other theories, educators have had to draw their own implications with respect to educational philosophy and practice.

Piaget has provided a conceptual framework and schema from which to view educational problems. It will be observed that many experimenters carrying out Piagetian studies have drawn educational implications from both the work of Piaget and their own investigations.

Arising from Piaget's theory, educators have placed increasing emphasis on the child being active in his learning, with the teacher's role involving stimulating the child to establish new levels of understanding. The teacher familiar with the stages is likely to be more appreciative of the disparity between language and thought, relative to the child's particular level of cognition. The importance of the early years for later cognitive growth is also realized as a result of Piaget's work, together with the important factor of the continuity of intellectual growth. Piaget's emphasis on social interaction as a necessary condition for cognitive growth has supported other influences in establishing learning situations in schools where pupils are encouraged to interact (Beard, 1969; Athey, 1970; Elkind, 1970; and Furth, 1970 together with others have further discussed the educational implications of Piaget's theory.)

However, Vinh-Bang (1971) draws a distinction between the interests of Piaget as he studies the child and those who would like to contribute directly towards change in the teaching-learning situation. He questions the practice of direct application of Piaget's research techniques into exercises for students and considers that this reveals a lack of understanding of developmental psychology. He concludes: 'The research of Piaget in developmental psychology has provided a theoretical foundation. It is left to us to project his theoretical models into the reality of the schools; in other words to make the solutions operational for the schools. In this way, the thought of Piaget will remain intact, yet his work will have a determining influence on the educational system.' (See also Boyle 1975, discussed earlier).

More recently, with the publication of *The Science of Education and Psychology of the Child* (1970) together with an article written for a series of studies prepared for the International Commission on the Development of Education, for Unesco (1972), Piaget has revealed an interest in the school curriculum. Within this sphere he reaffirms his approach to the development of intelligence as being of a 'constructivist nature (attributing the beginnings of language to structures formed by the pre-existing sensorimotor intelligence). It recognizes neither external preformations (empiricism) nor imminent preformations (innateness), but rather affirms a continuous surpassing of successive stages. This obviously leads to placing all educational stress on the spontaneous aspects of the child's activity.' Piaget draws attention to the proportionally small number of students following courses in science as opposed to liberal arts. He advocates a complete revision of methods and aims in education involving pre-school education — more active methods, the application of child and adolescent psychology and interdisciplinary curricula as opposed to 'compartmentalization'. He commends practice in observation at the pre-school level; more active methods which involve the child and adolescent learning every new truth by discovery and reconstruction with the teacher creating the situations and being 'a mentor stimulating initiative and research'. An approach to subjects from an interdisciplinary point of view, with more flexibility between the human and natural sciences and an upgrading of the teaching profession at all levels (to include a full university training and the acquisition of adequate psychological knowledge) are also recommended. Piaget is particularly appreciative of the primary teacher's role 'for the younger the students are, the more difficult the teacher's task, if it is taken seriously'.

Kohlberg (1972) views the Piagetian approach as a restatement of Dewey's progressive education but with a firmer grounding in empirical method. Kohlberg argued that the Piaget-Dewey philosophy is the axis around which American education should rotate.

Selman (1975) has argued, '. . . If Piagetian stages form an invariant sequence, we know that a child whose reasoning is generally concrete operational across a wide range of problems may be ready to move to formal operations. If our educational aim is to further the child's cognitive ability in the logical domain, our job is to develop activities with which the child can interact so that he may construct for himself the more adequate formal mode of reasoning. Similarly, the assumption of structural wholeness is important to the significance of Piaget's theory for education. If a child responds to one particular problem with formally operational thought, that in and of itself is of limited significance. But if the child's formally operational response to a specific problem generally indicates the child's thought organization (as the assumption of structural wholeness implies), this is far more significant. In other words, the assumption of structural wholeness implies that a Piagetian measure of logical reasoning has great predictive power from the problem at hand to other problems in the logical reasoning realm. Some observers have been skeptical of the possibilities of reinterpreting Piagetian developmental theory in terms of educational practice. For example, given that Piagetian stages represent a universal and invariant sequence in the development of cognition, some critics ask why something which will develop anyway should be taught. In fact, they ask whether one can teach or accelerate the emergence of developmental concepts or abilities at all. Furth and Wachs respond by noting that it is necessary to examine the role of variability in this theory. Universality of sequence does not imply that advancement through stages is predetermined. Experience plays a critical part in conceptual stage development. One way to clarify the role of experience within a theory of universal stage development is to recognize that certain forms of experience are universal across cultures . . . Yet although these forms of experience are culturally universal, individuals do not experience them in a predetermined manner. The provision of certain facilitating experiences can help children progress through a developmental sequence. The number and kind of experiences have an important effect on the rate and extent of development. Research, including Furth's previous study of deaf and blind children, supports the hypothesis of universality of logical thought sequence, while also sustaining the hypothesis of variability in rate of stage development. Finally, within each individual there is variation in level of reasoning depending on the concept or domain reasoned about. These aspects of structural developmental theory bear directly on education, indicating the potential of intervention using a Piagetian framework. Furth and Wachs argue cogently for the applicability of the theory', (p. 128–129).

Selman further argued that the most convincing implication of

Piaget's theory for education is that it supported the argument 'that some stages of thinking are more adequate than others, both philosophically and psychologically, and seeks to trace the development of these stages. But not all knowledge is subsumed under stage analysis. Furth and Wachs make a distinction between "Piagetian development" as representative of active thought or of reasoning process and "learning" as representative of basic fact or skill acquisition. They then introduce the concepts of high- versus low-level reasoning, relative to the child's own stage of development, to stress that activities need to stimulate thinking at a high-level. The teacher's task is to present activities with which each child can naturally interact and which can stimulate the child to move to the next level. Furth and Wachs also outline the educational implications of Piaget's concept of *décalage* which refers to an individual's operating at different cognitive stages at different times or in different realms. The concept is often employed in a defensive manner by some followers of Piaget to explain away differences in the way an individual reasons across various Piagetian tasks', (p. 129).

A functional (as opposed to structural) theory of intellectual development was presented by Case (1974) and used to generate specific performance models for Piagetian tasks involving the control of variables. On the basis of these models it was concluded that 'intelligent, field independent 7- and 8-year-olds should be able to acquire the control of variables scheme, even though they have not yet acquired either conservation of weight or the combinatorial system'. Preliminary data was presented to support this conclusion. They were discussed 'with regard to Piaget's formal theory of intellectual development, and the functional limitations of development on learning'. (Details are given later).

Case (1974a) sums very lucidly the proposed theory of Gagné (1968) and Pascual-Leone's (1975) model (the latter during the course of his doctoral work at Geneva utilized both the clinical data already available and additional data which he gathered himself). Case states, 'Gagné's theory takes account of the structural changes which occur in development, by proposing that learning is cumulative and hierarchical. Complicated skills can be acquired only once lower order component-skills have been mastered; furthermore, lower order skills are learned by processes which are qualitatively different from those by which higher order skills are learned. According to Gagné, instruction can be successful in improving performance on complicated developmental tasks, but only if it is based on a learning hierarchy analysis which breaks the criterion task into component tasks, and which trains each of these separately: working up from the simplest components to the most complex ones.

There are clear parallels between Gagné's model and Pascual-Leone's. Gagné's model interprets cognitive problems as requiring the application of certain rules. Pascual-Leone's model interprets these same problems as requiring the coordination of certain schemes (some of which are merely the internal representation of such rules). Gagné sees complex rules as being built up from simple rules, which are in turn, built up from concepts, and so on, down to the most basic "building blocks" which are S—R connections. Pascual-Leone sees complex schemes as being built up from more simple and less differentiated schemes which are in turn built up from simpler schemes still, and so on, down to the most basic "building blocks" which are Piaget's innate, stimulus-specific, motor schemes. Both theorists agree that children will not be able to solve cognitive problems if they do not have the appropriate internalized items of information in their repertoires. Both theorists agree that children can often be enabled to solve such problems if they are helped to acquire the appropriate repertoires, i.e., if they are instructed. The difference lies in the role assigned to the development. For Gagné, the process of development is largely one of cumulative learning, within the confines of whatever (unspecified) limitations may be imposed by "growth" (*cf.* Gagné, 1968). For Pascual-Leone, the process of development is equally one of cumulative learning. However, one of the major limitations imposed by "growth" is explicitly defined. It is a limitation in mental space', Case (*ibid.*, p.356).

In a study entitled, 'Mental strategies, mental capacity, and instruction: a neo-Piagetian investigation', Case therefore used Pascual-Leone's neo-Piagetian theory of development to predict the pre- and post-instruction distributions of scores on a subject-controlled digit placement task as a function of three parameters: the mental strategy which Ss attempted to apply; the demand which attempting to apply this strategy placed on their mental capacity; and the maximum mental capacity which they were capable of mobilizing. The results demonstrated that the predicted and obtained distributions corresponded closely for each kind of strategy. This held true at each age level sampled (six, eight, and 10). Case discussed the results focusing on the methodological and analytic requirements which must be satisfied if the same approach were to be applied to making successful predictions in more naturalistic paradigms. (Details are given later).

Case (1975) describes a series of studies which suggest that significant social class differences exist with regard to two of the factors found by neo-Piagetian theory to be necessary for performance on Piagetian tasks: the subjects repertoire of task-related schemes and the repertoire of general executive schemes. Lower class children did not appear to differ significantly from upper class children in their degree of field independence or in the size of their mental — space. (Details are given more appropriately in Volume 5 in the series, *Piagetian Research*.)

A pre-theoretical model of cognitive development has been proposed by Furby (1972) based on the empirical establishment of Gagné's cumulative learning sequences (*op. cit.*). She discussed in detail the application of the model to Piaget's conservation task and demonstrated the 'give-and-take' between empirical evidence and theoretical model building. (Details appear later).

The presentation of a conceptual hierarchy theory followed by a comparison of the theory with Staat's Behavioural Interaction Approach, Gagné's Cumulative Learning Model (*op. cit.*) and Piaget's Theory is made by Gander (1975) who asserted that the theory has aspects of both the behaviourist and cognitive viewpoints. 'It may be referred to as a cumulative learning theory of cognitive development in which learning is defined as the gradual organizing of information into concepts and hierarchical networks of concepts referred to as cognitive structure (not literally a network of connected concepts, concepts are "connected" in that one concept may call to mind another). It is hierarchical because the formation of many concepts requires the prior formation of subordinate concepts. The nature and formation of concepts are of central concern'. (Details appear later).

(See also Volume Four: *School Curriculum and Test Development* in the present series)

Abstracts

An interpretive framework of cognitive structures
W.M. Bart and M.B. Smith, 1974

The intention of the authors was to contribute to the structural analysis of cognitive development by providing a precise formulation of the generic notion of cognitive structure. They emphasize that developmental psychologists posit similar but not equivalent definitions of the term 'cognitive structure'; acknowledging that Piaget has provided one of the most exacting definitions, discussion is provided to show the inadequacies of the model.

An 'ordinary language *definition*' of cognitive structure involves a consideration of 'elements' and 'processes' together with a set of rules which are the relations among the processes, governing the order and forms of employment of the processes. Rules thereby provide axiomatic laws which allow for classification of cognitive structures, thereby establishing classes of cognitive structures that may be used to designate the Piagetian concept of period. In this framework, the mathematical theory of categories can be employed. (Full details of this theory are given by the authors, pp. 164–65).

Four assumptions basic to the framework are presented: 'the existing cognitive structure for any living organism is unique'; 'the periods of cognitive development form an inclusion chain', there is an invariant sequence of periods, so that present periods not only include the capabilities of previous periods but also have the potential capabilities of future periods; 'the cognitive structures for any living animal over time form an inclusion chain'; and 'the set of all cognitive structures manifested by an assemblage of living animals forms a semi-lattice with a common infinum'. The semi-lattice posited does not constrain each organism to follow an invariant path, but allows for somewhat individualized or idiosyncratic development.

'A fundamental conjecture of cognitive structures' can be obtained from the four assumptions: '(1) genetic components establish the maximal cognitive structure for an organism, the upper limit of the cognitive structures that may be manifested by an organism; (2) genetic components as well as environmental factors contribute substantially to the sequence of cognitive structure that may be manifested by an organism, and (3) interaction with the environment triggers or activates potential cognitive structures of an organism into operation.'

The authors further discuss applications to intelligence, learning and developmental sequence theory, together with delineating new directions for empirical studies in the cognitive developmental field to supplement their interpretive framework.

A developmental study of cognitive dissonance as a function of level of intellectual performance on Piagetian tasks
A. Biaggio, G.A. Wegner, and S.C. Simpson, 1973

Experiment One

AIM / The major hypothesis tested in all experiments was that predictions derived from dissonance theory should hold only for subjects who had reached at least the concrete operational level, but not for the preoperational children.

SUBJECTS / N = 48, from kindergarten, first and second grades.

METHOD / The Piagetian tests administered were (a) seriation, (b) conservation of liquids, (c) class inclusion, (d) conservation of number, (e) conservation of volume, (f) seriation on a verbal plane. Tasks (a), (b), (e) and (f) were patterned after Atwood (1969). Ss who were non-operational on the first four tasks were considered preoperational and those who demonstrated operativity on all six tasks were considered at the formal operations level. Children were then randomly assigned to one of the experimental conditions in a four-factor design with two levels of each variable: probability of detection (high and low), severity of threat (severe and mild), sex (boys and girls), and level of intellectual development (pre-operational and concrete). The experimental procedure was similar to that described in Biaggio and Rodrigues (1971). The procedure may be summarized in the following steps: (a) Piagetian tests, (b) Experimental manipulation of probability of detection and severity of threat through verbal instructions, (c) First ranking of the toys, (d) First compliance test, (e) Irrelevant task, (f) second ranking of the toys, (f) Second Compliance test.

Experiment Two

SUBJECTS / N = 60, from kindergarten, second, and third grades.

METHOD / The tasks of seriation on a concrete plane, conservation of liquids, conservation of volume, and seriation on a verbal plane were the same as in Atwood (1969). Children were categorized as either pre-operational or concrete operational. Children were then randomly assigned to the experimental conditions. 'All children were presented with a boring task which consisted of placing toothpicks into a glass, one at a time, for three minutes. They were then shown a vertical 10-centimeter line on a piece of a paper, on which they were to place an X, indicating how well they liked doing the task. It was explained to them that the higher they placed the X, the more they liked the task. The high dissonance group was shown a small balloon and told that they would have it for helping the E with the project (small reward). The low dissonance group was shown a Lego building block set, . . . , and told that they would receive it for helping out . . . The control group (no reward) was told nothing . . .', p. 190. Details are also given in Brehm's (1956) study on postdecisional dissonance, and Festinger and Carlsmith's (1959) study on the effects of magnitude of reward upon attitude reward.

Experiment Three

SUBJECTS / N = 60, from kindergarten, first and second grades.

METHOD / Piagetian tasks of class-inclusion, seriation on a concrete plane, conservation of volume, and seriation on a verbal plane was administered to categorize children as preoperational or concrete operational. 'The experimental manipulation involved three groups: (a) a high dissonance group in which S had to choose between two toys that were close in desirability (the toys ranked second and third on the first evaluation were used for the choice situation), (b) a low dissonance group in which the toy alternatives were not close in desirability (the toys ranked second and fifth on the initial evaluation were used in the choice situation), and (c) a "gift" group which acted as a control group (S was given a toy and so did not have to make a choice between two toys)', p. 193. (Fuller details are given in Biaggio, Wegner, and Simpson, 1973, pp. 193–194).

RESULTS / No significant differences were computed between preoperational and concrete operational children in terms of dissonance predictions. 'Data from experiment one, revealed significant sex differences in compliance with a prohibition, as well as interaction effects between sex and severity of threat, and between sex and probability of detection. Data from experiment three indicated that both preoperational and concrete operational Ss may experience dissonance', p. 175.

Has psychology anything to offer the teacher? *
D.G. Boyle, 1975

Integral to Boyle's Paper on the contribution of psychology to the practising teacher was an examination of the educational implications of the studies of childhood made by Piaget. Boyle was intent to investigate the claim made by many writers that Piaget's studies 'so illuminate the growth of the intellect that they provide a sure foundation on which to base the elementary school curriculum'.

In elaboration, the author considered that the discrepancy between Piaget's theories and the recommended practices that his followers claim to be based upon them, is so great that 'the recommendations might well be based on no part whatsoever of the Piagetian canon'. Boyle focused on the concept of 'equilibration' as the most crucial factor in development in terms of Piagetian theory and queries Piaget's role in establishing the importance of activity and exploration being vital components of the learning experience of children. He cited Ripple and Rockcastle (1964) for a collection of papers by educators who argue convincingly that improvements in teaching methods have come about as a result of modifications to the curriculum made as a direct result of studies of children's performance rather than indirectly as a result of Piaget's influence. It is observed by Boyle that ten years later the significance of Piaget's work for the school curriculum is still obscure. In support of this observation reference is made to Furth and Wachs (1974) and Schwebel and Raph (1974) (These have been described in Volume Four, in the present series *Piagetian Research*). Boyle considered that the exposition of Piagets' theory as it applies to education by Furth and Wachs is full of 'special pleading, misrepresentation of other viewpoints, and in some cases what appear to be blatant misunderstandings': illustrated through their interpretation of the educational system, examples of children's behaviour

---

* Gratitude is extended to Dr D.G. Boyle of the University of Aberdeen for sending his work to be abstracted.

and the relation between language and thinking respectively. (Further details appear in Boyle 1975, pp. 54–55.) Boyle continued that Furth and Wachs are even less plausible when they attempt to generalize their conclusions, he quoted, (Furth and Wachs, p. 23) '. . . the teacher must be firmly convinced that thinking cannot be taught as a subject matter and is not an object of knowledge that is remembered and can be forgotten. Piaget's theory provides the necessary framework that can give the teacher this reasonable assurance'. Boyle commented: 'of course thinking cannot be "subject matter" or "an object of knowledge". What need can there possibly be for a theory, Piaget's or otherwise, to buttress this banality?'.

Likewise, in Boyle's view, Schwebel and Raph present similar misrepresentations and in particular he objects to the given impression that only teachers committed to Piagetian theory are capable of being imaginative and stimulating the imaginations of the children they teach. 'It is the suggestion that all schools not following Piagetian precepts are harsh and unsatisfactory environments for the developing mind. This is a gross misrepresentation of education as we have known it for many years. Certainly the nature of schooling has changed since Victorian or even Edwardian times, but to attribute the changes to the influence of Piaget is to give Piaget credit that is due rather to Montessori'.

Boyle emphasized that Piaget himself has very little to say on the subject of education because he believes 'quite rightly', that educators must be free to base their practices on psychology without being bound by the conclusions of psychology. However, on the question of the nature of education, he is quite clear about the importance of activity. Following further discussion (pp. 56–57) Boyle summarized '"spontaneous" development is not spontaneous at all. Development depends upon environment, and it is up to the teacher to provide the right environment. Did teachers need to read Piaget to learn that?'

Boyle clarified that his main objection 'is to the almost religious ethos of the writings of those of Piaget's followers who can do him nothing but harm by falsely attributing to his influence changes that have come about as a result of other influences, and by recommending educational practices that, whilst they may be good in themselves, have only the most tenuous connection with Piaget's work'. In continuation: 'I foresee the day when a highly intelligent five-year-old, from a highly verbal home, will be hampered in his development by being forced to work through Piagetian exercises because Piaget acolytes refuse to accept that some children come to terms with the world verbally. Such dog in the manger attitudes are not uncommon among adherents of new philosophies, educational or otherwise'.

Following an analysis of Piaget's own claims with respect to his contribution in general (pp 58–59) Boyle concluded: 'Piaget's work provides the teacher with a comprehensive conceptual framework in terms of which he can analyse his techniques, and evaluate their outcomes. In this it is valuable, but it would be a mistake to regard it as anything more'.

Socio- and psycho-historical factors in the development and growth of a social-science, the impact of Jean Piaget on American developmental psychology as a case study
S. Brumer, 1975.

AIM / To look at the impact of Piaget and his theory on American developmental psychology.

SUBJECTS / Six different groups of developmental psychologists: four cohort groups defined by the year they received their PhD, a group of Piagetian researchers and a group of S–R researchers. The four cohort groups were defined as follows: (i) PhD obtained from 1926–1935; (ii) PhD obtained from 1936–1945; (iii) PhD obtained from 1946–1955; and (iv) PhD obtained from 1956–1965.

METHOD / 'A questionnaire' was sent to the Ss for completion and return.

RESULTS / The Piagetian researchers were observed to be a hybrid group, identifying with both the American and Piagetian definitions of development. Likewise, the Piagetian researchers and the researchers of cognitive development were younger psychologists, many of whom had been introduced to the new ideas during their graduate years. 'When change comes, it is usually in the problem area of research and not in theoretical orientation. If the change is in orientation, it often is followed by departure from the field. Further insights . . . of some of the changes in developmental psychology from 1950 to 1970 are obtained by a quantitative analysis of the growth of the field and by looking at quantitative and qualitative changes in the journal *Child Development*, considered to be representative of the literature of the field. These changes include a doubling of the literature every five to six years, an increase in the use of the experimental-manipulative approach, an increase in research based on theory and on Piagetian-related subjects, the predominance of studies on cognitive development and the secondary importance of socialization and affective variables.'

Mental strategies, mental capacity, and instruction: a neo-Piagetian investigation
R. Case, 1974a

AIM / Case used Pascual-Leone's neo-Piagetian theory of development to predict the pre- and post-instruction distributions of scores on a subject-controlled digit placement task as a function of the mental strategy which children attempted to apply; the demand which attempting to apply this strategy placed on their mental capacity; and the maximum mental capacity which they were capable of mobilizing.

Experiment One

SUBJECTS / N = 180, three different age groups with mean ages of six years 10 months, eight years 11 months, and 10 years 10 months.

METHOD / In the constrained version of the digit placement task, 'each S was first provided with a pre-training period of variable length, until he could easily place any number . . . in its correct spatial position with regard to an ordinal series of other numbers . . . After this pre-training, he was seated in front of an apparatus operated by the E, by means of which one number was exposed at a time. The E always exposed the ordinal series from left to right, at a rate of 1 number/1.5 sec. He then exposed the number to be placed, which was located at the far right-hand side of the apparatus. After this final number had disappeared, he asked the S to indicate where it belonged. Two blocks of five trials were presented. On the first, the total number of numbers presented per trial (n) was set equal to the modal number of schemes (k) which Ss of the particular age group in question were known to be capable of coordinating; that is, n was set at two for six-year-olds, three for eight-year-olds, and four for 10-year-olds. On the second block of five trials, n was set at k + 1. Under these conditions, it was shown that the M-demand of the task was within subjects' available M-space on the first five trials and one unit beyond it on the second five trials. In the modified (unconstrained) task developed for use in the present study, two changes were introduced: n was set at k + 2, and the operation of the apparatus was turned over to the S. The purpose of these changes was to present each S with an even greater potential capacity overload, as well as the opportunity to circumvent this overload by using an appropriate viewing procedure . . . Each S was informed that he could use any viewing procedure which he chose. The E then demonstrated several possible starting points . . .' (p. 384).

Experiment Two

METHOD /The protocol used with the left-right viewers who were assigned to the treatment condition was as follows: 'Would you like to learn a sneaky way of getting this problem right every time? You would? O.K. Now watch how I do this. First, I look at this number . . . Now I will have to remember it, so I'll say it again. What is it? . . . That's right, 15. Now, I start down here lifting each door. And I ask, is 8 bigger than 15? Is it? No. So I go on and ask, Is 11 bigger than 15? Is it? . . . No. So I go on and ask, Is 19 bigger than 15? Is it? . . . Yes. So I put the token down here. Now I know it's bigger than this number (11), but it's not bigger than this one (19), so it must be in the right place. See! (The E lifted the two doors for 11 and 19 at once) 15 comes in between 11 and 19. It's bigger than 11, and it's not bigger than 19. Now I want you to try it. Here, take this (token) and start' (pp. 390—391).

With the Ss in the control condition the protocol was as follows: 'Now we are going to give you some practice in the ones you got wrong, to see if you can get them right on a second try . . . Let's see if you can get this one right this time. If the child got it right the E said "Good! Now let's try another one." If the child got it wrong the E lifted the doors on either side of the token, together with the one concealing the number to be placed and said "Oh, Oh! Were you right? No, but let me give you another chance. Try again and see if you can figure out where this number really belongs . . . Now let's try another one!" ' (p. 384).

(Fuller details of the criterion measures, design and procedure, task analysis and predictions are described elsewhere, Case, 1974a, pp. 384—393).

RESULTS / Case concluded the results of both the experiments by stating that the neo-Piagetian theory has the potential 'to make detailed performance predictions in relatively unconstrained developmental problems, provided the possible mental strategies which a S might use can be clearly specified, and provided they can be conveniently assessed . . . the theory's greatest predictive potential probably lies in the area of instruction and development, since instruction on a developmental task can be conceptualized as a direct attempt to provide a S with a more sophisticated strategy than he presently uses, and one which it would take him a good many more years . . . to develop on his own . . . A careful task analysis must be conducted to determine the M-demand required to acquire . . . the strategy, and this analysis must take into account the possible effects of competing strategies and misleading cues' (p. 397).

Structures and strictures: some functional limitations on the course of cognitive growth
R. Case, 1974;

Case focused upon the structural predominance of Piaget's theory of intellectual development: he considered that developmental psychology needs a parallel theory which is predominantly functional, in order to achieve a greater degree of predictive power. A functional theory is one 'which describes the devices or mechanisms by which human knowledge is actually acquired and utilized.' The purpose of his article was to outline the general functional theory of cognition being developed by Pascual-Leone and his co-workers; to demonstrate that the theory is capable of generating detailed 'performance' models for a group of Piagetian tasks; 'to present some counter-intuitive data which are successfully predicted by these models and in the light of the data to reconsider the nature of developmental limitations on the acquisition of specific logical structures'.

Pascual-Leone's (1969) functional theory employs as its basic construct the Piagetian notion of a scheme. Schemes are defined as the subjective units of thought, that is, 'as the mental blueprints which represent experience and which are responsible for producing behaviour'. They are classified into three main categories: figurative, operative and executive. Figurative schemes are the internal representations of items of information with which a subject is familiar; operative schemes correspond to what Inhelder and Piaget have labelled 'transformations', the internal representations of functions (rules) which can be applied to one set of figurative schemes, in order to generate a new set; executive schemes are the internal representations of procedures which can be applied in the face of particular problem situations, in an attempt to reach particular objectives. (Further elaboration is given in Case, 1974, pp. 546—50). Case (pp. 550—59) sets down an 'explicit set of heuristics' whereby Pascual-Leone's theory may be used to generate a detailed performance model for a particular set of Piagetian tasks. On the basis of the models it was concluded that intelligent, field-independent seven- and eight-year-olds should be able to acquire the control of variables scheme, even though they have not yet acquired either conservation of weight or the combinational scheme. Preliminary data (N = 52) supported this conclusion. Case elaborates in answer to the query as to how 7—8-year-olds managed to acquire a preliminary grasp of the control of variables structure, that it can be explained in the distinction between an analysis which is purely structural and an analysis which also considers the operations by which structures are acquired and utilized. 'From a purely structural point of view, the control-of-variables scheme is indeed a formal one', however, from a 'functional-structure point of view, the same scheme could be considered either formal or concrete depending on the operations which were involved in its acquisition and utilization'.

The conclusion can therefore be generated 'that the acquisition of any particular item of knowledge does not depend on the match between the formal structure of that knowledge and the formal structure of the knowledge which the child already possesses. Rather, it depends upon the match between the pragmatic structure of the situation in which the child first has a chance to construct that particular item of knowledge and the functional limitations of his thought processes at the stage in his life when he first encounters such a situation'. Because Pascual-Leone's theory of development concentrates more heavily on functional mechanisms than does Piaget, it is capable of generating performance models of somewhat greater predictive power.

Critical contributions of Piaget to developmental Psychology*
R.N. Cassel, 1973

The many contributions made by Piaget to our understanding of human behaviour all deal with learning of the individual. For him learning and perception are different phenomena: perception involves a mental imagery of phenomena; while learning always involves the relating of that imagery to one's own past experience. Piaget maintains that how one relates the perceptions to past experience is directly related to four independently organized development stages — (1) sensorimotor, (2) pre-operational, (3) concrete operations, and (4) formal operations. While Darwin more than a half century earlier defined the process of natural selection which served to characterize the growth process, it was Piaget who described the stages for such adaptation in detail and with great precision, i.e. association, assimilation, accomodation, and aliment. Simultaneously, the affective element is more important in the domain of persons, and the cognitive element in the domain of things.

Examining Piaget's contributions in relation to humanistic psychology*
R.N. Cassel, 1975

According to Charlotte Bühler, Humanistic Psychology began in 1962 when A. Maslow in cooperation with a small group of colleagues founded the Association of Humanistic Psychology. Until this time systematic psychology was characterized by two main thrusts: (1) Behavioral psychology-externally conceived goals imposed on others, and (2) Dynamic psychology- unconscious defense mechanisms precluded self understanding. Humanistic psychology embraced the

---

* Written and prepared by the author for inclusion in this volume. Gratitude is extended to Dr Russel N. Cassel of Project Innovation, California.

notion that there was a natural tendency for growth that was determined from one's inner core and ranging to a new kind of religious self-integration into the cosmos. More than a half century before the founding of the Association for Humanistic Psychology Piaget in Switzerland was describing in considerable detail precisely the same principles espoused by the newly organized and espoused discipline. This evidence is overwhelming, and we must conclude that Piaget like Maslow is a Humanistic Psychologist.

Developmental and educational applications of Structure Theory: a mathematical reformulation of Piaget's concept of Structure*
D. Dirlam, 1975

In Piagetian theory the concept of structure is one of the most significant (Piaget, 1970; Gardner, 1972) but it's also one of the most elusive concepts for research and educational purposes. Over the last five years several co-workers and I have developed a mathematical method for classifying and evaluating structures that can be readily applied to problems in cognitive and developmental psychology, semantic, development, and the individualized evaluation of educational practices (Dirlam, 1972, 1973; Dirlam, Courtney, Uttich and Hays, 1974a; Dirlam, Mendez, Michal and Palm, 1974b; and Dirlam and Opitz, 1974c).

We begin with an inventory (1) of enordered items to be *organized* by a *structure*. The structures, then, are defined as labeled tree diagrams, which can differ in (1) the underlying *diagram*, (2) the set of labels used (called the glossary, G), (3) the method of labeling the nodes (resulting in *hierarchical*, *product*, or *power* structures), (4) the type of search (totally *left-ordered*, *partially ordered* random, and *blind*) and (5) the probability of scanning each node during the search (see Table 1). The *search length* ($_AL_S$) is the number of labeled nodes that need to be scanned in order to locate a particular item in the inventory. These preliminary definitions permit rather straightforward definitions of the concepts used to evaluate structures: (the average efficiency and power will be designated by $_AE$ and P, respectively) (1)

$$_AE+=\frac{1}{_AL_S} \quad (2) \quad p = \frac{1-1}{G}$$

and (3) flexibility refers to the ability to exchange levels in some structures without changing their efficiency of power (see the Appendix for further details).

---

* Published by the kind permission of the author.
Gratitude is extended to Dr David Dirlam of State University of New York, College of Arts and Science.

Structure theory can be used to analyse any group of open-ended answers by its application in the form of a structured-key-word analysis. This method assumes that the meaning of each word is represented by features and that these features are also representable by words. To determine the features used to answer a question a word-count is first made. Any word that is found several times in each of several different person's answers is called a common feature. A structure is then formulated by determining if there are non-trivial examples fitting an answer and not the feature (if not, the answer is a subclass of the feature and the two form a small part of a hierarchy) and if not, whether there are non-trivial examples fitting both the answer and the feature (if so, the answer overlaps with the feature and the two form a part of two levels in a product structure). Obviously, the best method of formulating a subject's structure is to have the subject answer the preceding questions. If this is not feasible (as for example when the structure must be determined in one experimental session), there are several independent means of checking the structure types used. Labels for hierarchies are generally easier to represent visually, can be used in fewer contexts, are easier to discover, and are less generative than labels for product structures.

The preceding means for identifying structure type statements are supported both by the mathematical theory of structures presented above and by the empirical studies of Dirlam *et al.* (1974a and 1974b). Most of the predictions of the structure theory presented here are also consistent with Piaget's findings. Nevertheless, in one case there is an important difference. According to Piaget, addition and multiplication of classes develop simultaneously. In terms of structure theory, addition of classes employs a two-level hierarchy while multiplication of classes uses a two-level product structure. Therefore, addition of classes should be more primitive ontogenetically than multiplication of classes. Lieterman and Dirlam (unpublished study, 1973) replicated Piaget's original studies with the same results but also included a group not previously used by Piaget. We hypothesized that the use of the adjective modifying the super class "wooden" in the "white" vs. "wooden" vs. "brown" beads problem) confused children, because adjectives usually reduce the class of objects referred to. In the addition problem, using green and yellow paper stars, two series of questions were asked: (1) to compare 'green stars' with 'stars' (instead of 'green stars' with 'paper stars'); and (2) to compare animals with cows (there were five cows and three rabbits). These versions did not have the confusing adjective and were answered correctly as much as two years before the others. Finally, we are now using structure theory to analyze such diverse characteristics as identity development, memory of daily activities, the child's concepts of children at an earlier or later stage of development than themselves, and the use of metaphors to stimulate abstract thinking. It is known that structuring is an important aid to memory for adults (Dirlam *et al.*, 1974a; Dirlam, Hays and Davidson, in preparation; also see Paivio, 1971). Our present work is designed to determine whether it is an effective aid for children. In addition much problem solving can be viewed as memory searching (see Posner, 1973) a task for which structure theory has obvious applications. If structuring can be shown to aid problem solving in children a more effective integration of the work of Piaget and the cognitive psychologists can be brought to bear on 'the science of education'.

APPENDIX: *A Further Description of Structure Theory*

A structure can be conceived as a labeled tree-diagram (see Table 1c), which is searched by locating a single appropriate node at each successive level. It can also be conceived as a labeled n-dimensional space, which is searched by first looking for an appropriate large division, then a subdivision, a sub-subdivision, etc. (see Figure 1 and Figure 2). A node (or division is an element of the diagram; a labeled node will be called a 'feature'; and the set of labels of a particular diagram will be called its 'glossary' (see Table 1a and 1b). Defining a structure by distinguishing between diagrams and labels is one of the central concepts of structure theory. Because of this distinction, structures can be evaluated not only in terms of searching efficiency but also in terms of two now precise evaluative characteristics: power and flexibility. The efficiency of the structure is the average number of searches needed to locate an appropriate last node (see Table 1d). Efficiency varies with the order (see Table 2a) and probability (Table 1e) of searching nodes and the number of branches under each node in the tree (*c.f.* Dirlam, 1972). The power of the structure is the number of terminal nodes divided by the number of labels used (Table 2b). Notice that the efficiency is dependent only on the branching structure of the tree-diagram and not on the labels of the nodes whereas power also depends on the labels of the nodes on the tree. It varies with the number of times a given label is used (compare Table 1ci with 1cci; it is assumed that a label can't be used in two branches immediately under the same node). The Tables present visual and symbolic examples. For verbal examples consider a library system with top levels, such as science (natural [physics, chemistry], social [psychology, sociology]), humanities (classics, [history, philosophy], fine arts [music, visual arts]). This system is less powerfully structured than one with science (textbooks [over 25-years-old, less than 25-years-old], original works [over 25, less than 25]), humanities (textbooks [over 25, less than 25], and original works [over 25, less than 25]). Notice in these examples the diagrams are identical and only the labels of the structures differ. The efficiency of these two systems is identical if each searching route is equally probable. For example, if we assume that the search proceeds from left to right and then from top to bottom (a totally ordered search), then to find a book classed under (history), in the first structure the route would be (science), (humanities), (classics), (history) and the length of the search would be four nodes. If all of the nodes are equally likely to be searched then the average searching length (the efficiency) for this structure would be 4½. The only difference between the preceding structure and the one using (textbooks), (over 25), etc. is the labels of the nodes. The searching length for a humanities textbook over 25-years-old would be four as the analogous example above and the average if all searches in this structure are equally probable is 4½. The possible diagrams, on the other hand differ significantly. Thus the diagram in Table 1ai could be for either a product structure or a hierarchy but the diagram in Table 1aii could only be for a hierarchy. Furthermore, the power of the two types of structures differs very much. In both cases, the number of terminal nodes is 8, but in the first structure there are 14 different labels (the power equals 8/14) and in the second there are only 6 (P=8/6). If the first structure is continued by making binary divisions of each node and giving each new node a distinct label the efficiency will be 1 1/2 times the number of levels and the power will approach 1/2. If the second structure is continued by making binary division of each node but giving the same pair of labels to each division in a level, the efficiency will be 1 1/2 times the number of levels as before but the power will almost double with each new level. Notice also that the order of levels is fixed in the first type of structure but not in the second. Thus, it would be extremely inefficient to look for a book under 'physics' if it had not been determined that the book is 'scientific', but it would be just as appropriate to look under 'less than 25-years-old' first as to look under 'science' first. This property of the latter structure will be referred to as its flexibility (see Table 2c). Also, it should be noted that only the second type of structure is generative. A distinction of the first type adds only 1, 2, 3, etc. items depending on whether it is bi-, tri-, quadri-, etc. partite while a division of the second type multiples the number of items by 2-, 3-, 4-, etc. times. Finally, the first type of structure, in which each label is used for only one node, will be called a 'hierarchy' (as in Table 2ci). The second type of structure can be more easily defined by introducing the concept of a 'bush', which is the set of nodes branching from exactly one node on the previous level. This latter structures, then is one in which any bush in any given level of the structure contains the same number of nodes and is labeled with exactly the same set of labels as all the other bushes in that level.

Because of its resemblance to the n-dimensional cartisian product, it will be called a 'product structure' (see Table 2cii, it also resembles the structure Posner, 1973, refers to as a 'space').

Table 1. The variety of structures.

(a)   Two tree diagrams:

(i) 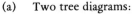   (ii)

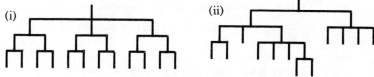

(b)   Two glossaries: (a,b,c,d,e,f,g,); (a,b,c, ... t,u).

(c)   Two methods of labeling a diagram resulting in two structures:

      (i)   A hierarchy.

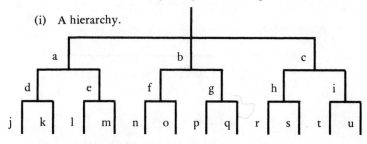

      (ii) A product structure.

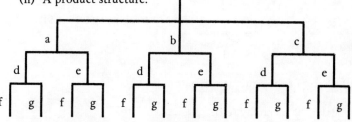

(d)   Four searches for q in the hierarchy above (c,i):
      (i)   The totally left-ordered search: <a,b,f,g,p,q,>.
      (ii) A partially ordered search: <a,c,b,f,g,q>.
      (iii) A random search: <a,c,a,b,f,g,p,q>.
      (iv) A blind search: <a,b,c,b,f,f,g,p,q,p,p,q,>.

(e)   Two sets of node probabilities:
      (i)   All nodes equally probable;
      (ii) All non-terminal nodes equally probable and the probability of terminal nodes Poisson distributed.

Table 2 Evaluation of structures in Table 1

(a) Efficiency of the average search for equally probable items:

    (i) Totally left-ordered search in the hierarchy (a,i):

$$_A E = \frac{12}{\dfrac{1}{12}(3+4+4+5+4+5+5+6+5+6+6+7)} = \frac{12}{5} = 2.4$$

    (ii) Partially ordered search in the hierarchy (a,i):

$$_A E = \frac{12}{\dfrac{1}{12}(12(2.0+1.5+1.5))} = \frac{12}{5} = 2.4$$

    (iii) Totally left-ordered search in the hierarchy (a,ii):

$$_A E = \frac{12}{\dfrac{1}{12}(3+4+3+5+6+7+9+10+3+4+5+6)} \simeq 2.2$$

    (iv) Partially ordered search in hierarchy (a,ii):

$$\frac{12}{_A E} = \frac{1}{12}(2(1.5+2+1.5)+(1.5+2)+3(1.5+2+2.5)+$$

$$2(1.5+2+2.5+1.5) + 4(1.5+2.5))$$

$$\simeq 5.2$$

$$_A E = 2.3$$

(b) Power of the structures in part c:

    (i) The hierarchy (c,i): $p = \dfrac{11}{21} \simeq 0.52$

    (ii) The product structure (c,ii): $P = \dfrac{11}{7} \simeq 1.57$

(c) Flexibility
    (i) Changing levels 1 and 2 of the diagram in a,ii is impossible regardless of how it is labeled.

Table 2 cont'd.

(ii) Exchanging labels 1 and 2 in the hierarchy (c,i) alters the glossary size by one and requires a change in the meaning labels because the same set of labels cannot be grouped together. The following preserves the vertical groups as much as possible:

(iii) Exchanging levels 1 and 2 in the product structure (c,ii) does not alter the efficiency, power, or the labels which appear in the vertical groups. This is illustrated in the following structure:

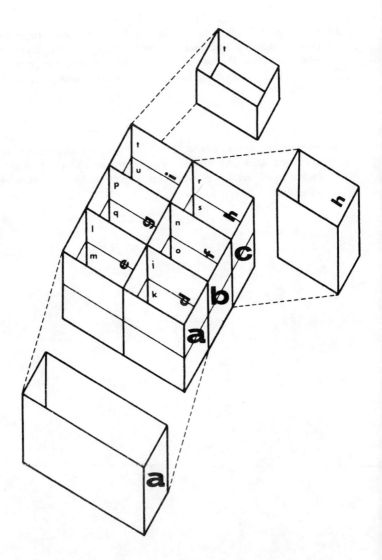

Figure 1.

A hierarchical method of labeling a spatial diagram. Notice that there are three levels of the hierarchy exactly analogous to the structure in Table 1ci with a—c representing classes, e—i representing sub-classes and j—u representing sub-sub-classes.

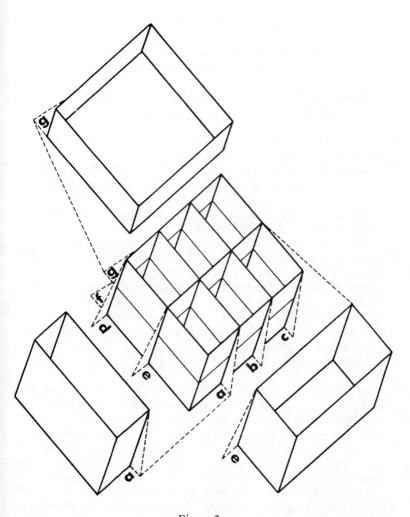

Figure 2

A product method of labeling the spatial diagram in Figure 1. Notice first that, like Table 1cii, each level contains only 2 or 3 classes that divide the whole space and secondly that levels are distinguished by the dimension of the division instead of by the portion of the whole being divided (as in Figure 1) so that a—c divide the whole along one dimension, d—e another and f—g a third.

A longitudinal study of Piaget's developmental stages and the concept of regression I
S.Z. Dudek and G.B. Dyer, 1972

AIM/ A longitudinal study was undertaken to study the Piaget's developmental stages and the concept of regression.

SUBJECTS/ N = 65 with an age range from five to nine years. Children with IQs below 80 and severe pathology were excluded.

METHOD/ All children were seen individually at yearly intervals for three consecutive years. The tests comprised:
  (a) The Weschler Intelligence Scale for Children (Weschler, 1949)
  (b) The Elementary School Personality Questionnaire (Cattell and Coan, 1966)
  (c) The Lorge-Thorndike Group Test of Intelligence (administered in the fourth year of the research only).
  (d) Piagetian tests comprised: (i) Notions of space and position in space; (ii) Age — measuring concepts of relative age, size and order of birth; (iii) Conservation of substance and weight; (iv) Conservation of area; (v) Origin of right, measuring concepts of causality; (vi) Origin of dreams also measuring concepts of causality; (vii) Class-inclusion; (viii) Two directions of orientation; (ix) Seriation and ordinal correspondence. (Details of the tests appear in Pinard and Laurendeau, 1962 and Dudek *et al.*, 1969).
  (e) The Rorschach Inkblot Test

RESULTS/ The authors conclude, 'Analysis . . . over a four year period on tests of operational and causal thinking offers support for Piaget's notion of stage progression. Over a three year period there were only eight true regressions; that is regressions from terminal stages to the initial or preparatory stage of operational and causal thinking. This constitutes only 6.5 per cent of the total number of actual regressions made and less than one per cent of the total of possible regressions for this period. Both the Piaget scores and the WISC measures were slightly higher for the regression children, but the numbers are too small to warrant any conclusions. However, they serve to demonstrate that "regressing children", . . . are not less intelligent than non-regressing children', p. 388.

An analysis of cognitive-developmental sequences
J.H. Flavell, 1972
The major objective of Flavell's monograph was to offer some proposals

concerning the classification and explanation of developmental sequences of cognitive acquisitions. It includes a brief discussion of 'What an "interesting" cognitive-developmental sequence might consist of and of some of the methodological problems that may complicate its empirical validation'. A classification system for such sequences was proposed : according to this system, 'if an earlier developing cognitive element (Skill, concept, etc. — "item" was the generic term used) is related in any meaningful formal or causal way to a later-developing one, thereby defining an "interesting" sequence, then the relationship between them can be described as one of developmental Addition, Substitution, Modification, Inclusion, or Mediation'. (Explanation of these terms is given in Flavell, 1972, pp. 287–317).

Flavell further examined the problem of explaining invariant or near-invariant cognitive-developmental sequences. It was proposed that any sequence would best be explained by appeal to one of three factors: the structure of the organism, the structure of the environment and the structure of the items. Flavell considered that some sequences may finally prove to be explicable only by recourse to 'some sort of biological-maturational account'. The developmental attainment of certain cognitive items may occur largely through repeated contacts with certain classes of environmental inputs, for instance 'interpersonal knowledge and skills being acquired through repeated experiences with other human beings'. The structure of these inputs may make highly probable the acquisition of one cognitive item prior to the acquisition of another. Some sequences may be accounted for 'simply by the fact that if we hold to our current theoretical definitions of the two items, the reverse sequence is logically impossible. If, for example, one item is included in the very definition of another but not vice versa (as concrete operations are included in Piaget's definition of formal operations without the converse being true), then the latter could not develop prior to the former'.

Flavell proposed the following strategy for attempting to explain any prospective sequence: (a) first, see if the sequence is explainable by item-structure (logical) considerations alone, . . . ; (b) if not, see if a plausible environment-structure explanation can be found, and if so, accept it at least provisionally; (c) if not, assume *faute de mieux* and very tentatively — that our species may simply be biologically programmed through evolution to develop those particular cognitive items in that particular order'.

Flavell further argued that human cognitive growth may exhibit significant asequential features in addition to the obvious sequential ones and that a realistic, balanced view of such growth should take account of both sorts of features.

Cumulative learning and cognitive development
L. Furby, 1972

The author focused upon Gagné's cumulative model of human intellectual development which has contributed toward the understanding of the nature of the relation between learning and development. Gagné has contrasted his model to those emphasizing maturational readiness or cognitive adaptation (Piaget) and instead suggests that intellectual development depends mainly upon the acquisition of 'an ordered set of capabilities which build upon each other in progressive fashion though the processes of differentiation, recall and transfer of learning' (Gagné, 1968, p. 181). Furby's paper dealt with the major example Gagné employed in order to demonstrate the applicability of his model: Piaget's conservation task. Furby considered that 'in analyzing the conservation problem ambiguously and/or incorrectly, Gagné may have undermined both the understanding and the acceptance of what appears to be a potentially far-reaching model'. Furby attempted to clarify the nature of the conservation task and the implications of Gagné's model for understanding the intellectual development leading to success on such a task. Her first goal was thus to prevent rejection of the model itself due to the misleading analysis of the conservation task which was the primary example of the applicability of the model. She then devoted the major portion of her paper to a 'proposed pretheoretical model of cognitive development based essentially upon empirically established cumulative learning sequences'. While the model was general, it was discussed extensively 'in relation to the specific cognitive development involved in the conservation task performance, thus permitting (a) direct comparison to Gagné's analysis, and (b) use of the abundant empirical data available'. The final portion outlined 'the applicability and implications of such pretheoretical model building for both experimental research and theory (particularly Piaget) in cognitive development'.

Conceptual hierarchy theory: a theory of cognitive development
M.J. Gander, 1975

Conceptual hierarchy theory was presented and explained in detail followed by a comparison of the theory with Staat's Behavioural Interaction Approach, Gagné's Cumulative Learning Model, and Piaget's Theory.

The author maintained that conceptual hierarchy theory has aspects of both the behaviourist and cognitive viewpoints. 'It may be referred to as a cumulative learning theory of cognitive development in which learning is defined as the gradual organizing of information into concepts and hierarchical networks of concepts referred to as cognitive structure (not literally a network of connected concepts, concepts are "connected" in that one concept may call to mind another). It is hierarchical because the formation of many concepts requires the prior formation of subordinate concepts. The nature and formation of concepts are of central concern. "Concept" is a hypothetical construct used to represent the form into which information is organized and stored in the human brain. Information may be sensory data or symbolic. Two fundamental types of concepts are: (1) identity concepts, those which represent a particular object, place, event, relationship, living thing, etc., and (2) rules or class concepts, those which represent the commonality(ies) across two or more identities or other classes ... Concept formation is a gradual process which may take several years. It may be facilitated through the use of strategies. Strategies are concepts which organize information about ways of going about organizing information ... A fundamental assumption is that the universe is "logical" ... Another basic assumption of the theory is that cognitive content can be "called to mind" by various stimuli. Explication of how this is possible remains incomplete. The answer may well lie in biochemistry and neurophysiology.'

Cognition and the acquisition of selected function words in poverty children
M.L. Hanes, 1974

AIMS / Hanes reviews the contributions of Brown (1973) and Piaget (1926) on language and cognitive development and hypotheses, were derived 'which specifically considered the acquisition of selected function words, including three classes of subordinate connectives and the prepositional phrase in the reversible passive construction. Temporal, causal, and antithetical connectives were the three subordinate connective classes studied. The hypotheses predicted an order of acquisition for connective classes, for connective forms within a class, and a sequence of approximations to the correct response to the prepositional phrase in the passive construction'.

SUBJECTS / Three groups of poverty children : black inner city, white rural, and bilingual Puerto Rican. Samples were drawn from three age levels: six-, seven-, and eight-year-old children.

METHOD / Each subject was tested individually on a sentence

repetition task which comprised 28 stimulus sentences. The responses were tape recorded and scored for function word omissions, substitutions, errors, and verbatim repetitions.

RESULTS / Temporal connectives were acquired prior to causal and antithetical connectives. 'Also, causals are acquired prior to antitheticals ... the results support the proposition that the differentiation of forms within a class does not occur simultaneously with the acquisition of a connective class. Significant differences between subcultural groups were associated primarily with the bilingual Puerto Rican group. These differences were attributed to the delayed language development that bilingual children exhibit. It was suggested that the most significant aspect of this study was that data was obtained from two unique research samples. These data provide a basis for future investigations of the language acquisition process in white rural and bilingual poverty children.'

If you want to get ahead, get a theory
A. Karmiloff-Smith and B. Inhelder, 1975

AIM / An attempt to understand children's processes of discovery in action. Inhelder, Sinclair and Bovet (1974) illustrated the 'dynamics of interstage transitions' together with the 'interaction between the child's various subsystems belonging to different developmental levels.' However, experiments are still lacking with respect to children's spontaneous organizing activity in goal-oriented tasks with little intervention from the experimenter, with particular focus on the 'interplay between action sequences and children's "theories-in-action", i.e., the implicit ideas or changing modes of representation underlying the sequences.' The block-balancing experiment is an initial attempt among a more comprehensive set of current studies (listed in Karmiloff-Smith and Inhelder, pp. 211–12) to study goal-oriented behaviour, specifically 'the interplay between action sequences and theories-in-action.'

SUBJECTS / N = 67 children aged from 4.6 to 9.5 years from a Geneva middle class school. Phase I included 44 subjects, 23 being interviewed again in Phase II. Five young subjects between 18 and 39 months were observed in 'provoked play sessions' with the blocks.

METHOD / 'Subjects were requested to "balance so that they do not fall" a variety of blocks across a narrow bar, i.e., a 1 x 25 cm metal rod fixed to a piece of wood.' There were seven types of blocks with several variants under each type. (Full details are given in Karmiloff-Smith and Inhelder, pp. 196–199.) 'Type A blocks had their weight evenly distributed; B blocks consisted of two identical overlapping blocks glued together, weight being evenly distributed in each block. In A and B blocks, the center of gravity thus coincided with the geometric centre of the length of the solid as a whole.' C types consisted of a block glued to a thin piece of plywood; D types were similar with the exception of the thicker plywood; E blocks were invisibly weighted with metal and F types contained a cavity at one end into which small blocks of various weights could be inserted. An "impossible" G block could not be balanced without counterweights.

In phase I, subjects were left free to choose the order in which they wished to balance each block, in order to gain insight into the spontaneous ways children endeavor to understand the properties of the blocks. Phase II involved interviewing half of the subjects twelve months later in order to verify the interpretative hypotheses and to determine progress. Further, to intervene more systematically by providing 'increased opportunity for positive and negative action – and theory-response, in order to study their interplay'. Situations were purposely chosen in which physical, spatial and logical reasoning was involved but which had already been 'analyzed from a structural point of view, thus providing additional means for interpreting data.'

RESULTS / The authors comment that action sequences are not merely a reflection of the child's implicit theories: 'the very organization and reorganization of the actions themselves, the lengthening of their sequences, their repetition and generalized application to new situations give rise to discoveries that will regulate the theories, just as the theories have a regulating effect on the action sequences.'

Positive and negative action – and theory-responses seem to have varying roles at different times. While the child is success-oriented positive action-response is important, successful actions are repeated. Negative action-response causes the child's attention to change to the means, e.g. 'how to balance' involving experimentation in order to seek knowledge of the approximate range of possible actions on an object. 'As the child gradually begins to construct a theory for interpreting the regularity of positive action-responses, these become positive theory-responses. Negative responses remain action-responses until the child's theory is generalized and consolidated, after which they progressively become negative theory-responses, once the child becomes aware of their regularity. A further important fact is that younger subjects make use of proprioceptive information in an uncontaminated fashion since they have not yet developed a unifying theory. For the more advanced subject the object's "behaviour" is evaluated conceptually, and they are only able to use the proprioceptive information if they close their eyes'. (Full discussion of the results are given in Karmiloff-Smith and Inhelder, pp. 200—210.) Results generally indicate that constructing and extending a 'powerful theory-in-action is a very general aspect of discovery which has a deeprooted function.' (A discussion of 'functional rather than structural analogies between the acquisition of physical knowledge and the acquisition of language' is included on pp. 209—210.)

Interactional aspects of cognitive organization
J. Langer, 1975

Langer (1975) makes further propositions towards a 'comprehensive structural developmental theory of cognitive change' begun in earlier works (Langer 1969a, 1969b).

Langer clarifies that his approach focuses upon 'intrinsic disequilibrium' as a source of the development and interiorization of mental operations (Langer, 1969b). This involves the exploration of the function of 'interactive disparity between intrinsic (organismic) and extrinsic (environmental) functional structures' which may perturb the existing cognitive organization of the child. It involves 'studying how interactive disparity may provide the occasion for perturbative feedback and the intrinsic disequilibrium necessary for conceptual transformation to a more advanced stage.' Efforts have been in part directed towards the distinction theoretically and empirically between 'external disparity' and 'intrinsic disequilibrium'. 'The equilibration model implies the hypothesis of progressive or regressive cognitive transformation when intrinsic disequilibrium or disparity has been demonstrated by independent means. Only then does the theoretical expectation follow that the energetic conditions are present for the formation and interiorization of more or less advanced mental operations and concepts.'

In an attempt to analyze intrinsic disequilibrium 'two major theoretical parameters of equilibrating intrinsic functional structures were proposed, an organizational and an energetic parameter (Langer, 1969b). An additional distinction was then made between two complementary aspects of the organizational parameter. The first is the interaction between the organism's systems of action, and the second is the interaction of the media in which acts and the environment are embodied.' Langer (1975) directs his Paper towards further analyses of these interactive aspects of equilibration.

Langer explores the transformational consequences of intrinsic interaction between two classes of functional structures: 'accommodatory figurations and assimilatory operations'. Further, the organizational issue, namely, 'to determine the results of interaction between functional structures for the formation of any given functional structure' and the developmental issue: 'to determine whether the results of interaction lead to some change, whether progressive or regressive, in any given functional structure.'

Four sections of the Paper outline some of the ways in which Langer has been investigating the problem experimentally. Each section is devoted to the discussion of 'one figurative means of mentally extracting or representing empirical information about physical and social objects and the consequences of such empirical activity for the construction of operational concepts. The first three figurative means are primarily extractive. They are imitating an observed event, comparing one's predictions about the result of a physical deformation with one's observation of the actual outcome and comparing one's observations of the way things appear with one's observations of the way things really are. The fourth figurative means is primarily representational and involves symbolization of empirical presentations and reasonings about them,' (pp. 14 – 24).

Among the educational implications of the findings Langer discusses the apparent discrepancy between the 'genotypical potential for cognitive development and its phenotypical actualization'. He focuses on the small proportion of people who progress to the level of principled morality and formal operations in logical development and further to the variation in rate of progress between cultures. The educational conclusion appears to be not to focus upon acceleration of developmental progress but the actualization of adolescents' genotypic potential for formal logical and principled moral thinking and action. 'A promising approach is to build upon the adolescents' competence to benefit from active verification procedures and his intrinsic state of structural disequilibrium.' The kind of education adolescents receive can be predicted to have a great effect upon their development – particularly the actualization of their potential for the final stages of the developmental sequence.

Piaget's questions to young children: an analysis of their structure and content
C.F. Palfrey, 1972

AIM / The author was intent 'to discover whether the child's developing conception of the world could be inferred from the answers given to questions based on Piaget's questioning of children'.

SUBJECT / N = 50, within the age range three to 11 years.

METHOD / Subjects were asked questions similar to or exactly the same as those reported by Piaget (1929) in *The Child's Conception of the World*. Briefly, the questions were as follows:

(a) 'Does the moon move?' (Piaget, 1929, p 147)
(b) 'Where do we come from?'
(c) 'Where do you come from?'

(Neither of those questions (b) and (c) are Piagetian.)

(d) 'What is "being happy"?' 'This question is similar in its construction and questioner's expectation to Piaget's "What is a thought"?'
(e) 'Tell me a strong word'. 'Here Piaget (1929, p. 45) has deliberately set out to inquire whether the child is able to dissociate the "thing" from the word which symbolizes it, or whether he believes in word magic', p. 126.
(f) 'Where do you think?' 'Piaget's question was "What do you think with?" ' (1929, p. 39) ' "Where do you think?" is a less limiting, more ambiguous question designed to add to the different forms of enquiry used in the present study', p. 127.
(g) 'What is a thought?' (Piaget, 1929, p. 50)
(h) 'Where do you dream?' 'Piaget's question was "Where do dreams come from?" ' (1929), p. 89 and p. 93)
(i) 'Where does the wind come from?' 'This is based on the structure of Piaget's question, "Where do dreams come from?" ', p. 129.
(j) 'Who made the wind?' (Piaget, 1929, p. 256).

RESULTS / Palfrey concludes, 'The responses to the ten questions put to the sample of children aged three to 11 . . . do not necessarily invalidate Piaget's hypotheses concerning the child's conception of the world. They do, however, cast doubt on the interview as an efficient method of clarifying our knowledge of the child's perception of and attitude towards external phenomena and his own self. The answers that children give to questions depend on the structure of the questions . . . it is not justifiable to judge the child's conception of the world as naive or uninformed, animistic or egocentric; nor can we state with any degree of certainty that children are unable to distinguish words from the ideas or objects they represent', p. 130.

Dialectic operations: the final period of cognitive development
K.F. Riegel, 1973

Riegel demonstrated that dialectic conceptualization characterizes the origin of thought in the individual and in society. Further, he considered that dialectic conceptualization represents 'a necessary synthesis in the development of thought toward maturity'.

He elaborated the implications for developmental psychology of the notion of 'dialectic interpenetration' and of the 'dismissal of the identity principle'. He recognized the dialectic basis of Piaget's theory, most clearly revealed in the accommodation-assimilation paradigm leading to adaptation and readaptation, but emphasized that critics have often wondered how the accommodation-assimilation paradigm is carried forward into the interpretations of the higher stages of cognitive development. Riegel considers that as Piaget's theory progresses to higher levels it becomes antidialectic and the 'progress of the child as described by Piaget is one of increasing alienation of thought'.

Riegel summarized that 'Piaget's theory describes thought in its alienation from its creative, dialectic basis. It represents a prototype reflecting the goals of our higher educational system which, in turn are reflecting the non-artistic and non-creative aspects in the intellectual history of Western man. Although Piaget's theory is founded on a dialectic basis, it fails to make the transition from the formal intellectualism of Kant to the concrete dialecticism of Hegel. Thus, his theory is not only incapable of interpreting mature thinking but, in his interpretation, also the cognitions of children (increasing with age) lose their dialectic and, thus, their creative character. A commitment to Hegel enables us to reinterpret Piaget's theory with due consideration of mature and creative thinking. It leads us to an extension and modification of Piaget's model of cognitive progression'.

Riegel elaborated that dialectic operations represent mature thought to which an individual might progress from any one of the four stages in Piaget's theory, i.e. without necessarily processing first through all four of them in their proper order. This further implies that an individual might perform in one area of concern at one level of thinking and in another area at another level. Riegel's modification and extension of Piaget's theory to the level of dialectic operations further implied concern with intrapsychic processes: the interaction between psychic activities and their biological basis and further, the interaction between psychic activities and the cultural-historical conditions.

Riegel concluded that the ceaseless striving toward formal operations becomes inappropriate and ineffective for the level of dialectic maturity, for they fail to represent adequately the thought and emotions of mature and creative persons.

Exposition, analysis and implications of selected presuppositions inherent in Piaget's theory
P.A. Tursi, 1973

AIM / The study attempted 'to analyze selected "organismic" presuppositions inherent within Piaget's theory of the ontogenesis of human scientific thought in order to discuss the epistemological consequences of these presuppositions'.

METHOD / The mode of analysis comprised such features as: exposition or presentation of Piaget's own ideas in his own terminology; analysis with a view to examination and interpretation; epistemological and ontological aspects of the presuppositions; and implications for childhood education. Presuppositions were analyzed via : (a) the 'world view' level or metaphysical system with the organism as the sort metaphor; (b) the 'paradigm' level using the historico-critical approach to theory construction, the paradigm of the natural scientist comprising five biological presuppositions, and three metatheoretical 'organismic' presuppositions; and (c) the theoretical level of Genetic Epistemology.

RESULTS / 'Piaget's acceptance of the biological organism as his sort metaphor is consistent with the "Holist" presupposition. The epistemological consequence is a coherence theory of truth which entails the belief that eclecticism has pitfalls and a rationale should be based upon a coherent position. It was assumed that any position accepting coherence and negating eclecticism would imply a "world view". Past analysis of the "organismic" world view accepted "objective idealism" with an absolute as an ideal end point for develop-ment . . . (the) author felt that the "relativism" presupposition comprised the superordinate construct in Piaget's system. The epistemological consequence is a relativistic epistemology. The central question of prime theoretical concern became, "How does one subjectively arrive at an objective view of reality?". If Piaget's version of the "organismic" world view can be interpreted as "objective relativism", one can legitimately claim to be a relativist and yet expect to achieve an objective view of the world, but it requires the surrender of the absolutist presupposition. The world view of "objective relativism" was then seen as compatible with Piaget's use of the sort metaphor of the biological organism, once the concepts final cause and teleology could be discarded. This permitted the use of an organismic position which accepted biological presuppositions consistent with the cybernetic models of Von Bertalanffy and Waddington. These were: (1) epigenesis, (2) evolution, (3) chreods, (4) homeorhesis, and (5) teleonomy. This led to the acceptance of a third organismic presupposition — dialecticism — with the epistemological consequence of constructivism. Constructivism is a new epistemology . . . whatever characteristic is revealed by an object under any specified conditions of observation is a real characteristic of it under those conditions . . . we can know its true nature despite these relativities . . . This, then, is how Piaget can attempt to explain how one subjectively constructs objective reality . . . Since Piaget's "world view" appears to be incompatible with the dominant world view extant in academic psychology and psychological foundations of education, it is not surprising that it is misunderstood'.

Catalogue of the Jean Piaget Archives
University of Geneva, 1975

Professor Bärbel Inhelder, Secretary of the Jean Piaget Archives Foundation, has provided the following information about the *Catalogue,* as publicized by G. K. Hall and Company publishers. Jean Piaget has been a pioneer in the study of intellectual growth and concept development in children. Biologist, philosopher, historian of science as well as psychologist, his work has always been inspired by deep reflection on the nature of scientific enterprise and on the problems of the growth of knowledge and the development of ideas. It is easy, therefore, to appreciate the great value of the creation of the Jean Piaget Archives in the Ecole de Psychologie et des Sciences de l'Education at Geneva, established with the support of the Swiss National Foundation for Scientific Research, the Academic Society of Geneva, the University of Geneva and the family of Jean Piaget. These Archives will play a fundamental role in all research on the history of psychology. They offer a rich documentation on a period, a person and a school decisive in formulating the key questions of psychology in the last 50 years.

The *Catalogue of the Jean Piaget Archives* is arranged in three sections. The first section contains the works of Piaget from 1907 to 1974; including all his scientific work and many other items bearing on educational, religious, philosophical and social questions. The earliest entry is "An albino sparrow", published in 1907. It is the first in a collection of about 1500 titles: manuscripts, articles, books, monographs, prefaces, commentaries, and responses. The original works as well as their translations are included. The second section of about 400 items contains the works of some of Piaget's immediate collaborators. The third section brings together the secondary literature stimulated by the work of Piaget. The *Catalogue* now lists about 1,000 titles, representing the most important works to date. Each card in the *Catalogue* contains a full bibliographic citation. Items are arranged in chronological order within each section. There are approximately 4,000 cards in this catalogue.

Piaget's work in early child development as it relates to Chomskian psycholinguistics
G.L.S. Von-Hippel 1972

'Piaget's theory of early child development is related to some of the psycholinguistic issues raised by Chomsky's syntactic theory. Several requirements are suggested for an adequate account of language acquisition. It must describe the phonological, semantic and syntactic organization of the child . . . it must explain the facts that a child can acquire any language, that a child acquires a particular language, and that there is some biological predisposition for this acquisition. Other facts, suggested in the psycholinguistic literature as requiring explanation, are the rapidity and complexity of language acquisition. These are disputed.'

'Piaget's contention is that language is one kind of symbolic activity. Piaget defines symbolic functioning as the use of differentiated signifiers — signs and symbols — to evoke absent significates. Symbolic functioning and representation are identical for Piaget. His account of early language development is portrayed as inadequate to explain the specifics of early language acquisition.'

'Piaget claims that language differs from other symbolic activity by virtue of the representative medium involved and is similar to other symbolic activity by virtue of the cognitive structures into which this representative medium is integrated. The author agrees with the Chomskian view that this claim is unjustified. Piaget, like others who hold a similar position, does not present a sufficiently detailed description of the cognitive organization of different symbolic activities to justify the conclusion that they are similar.'

'It is suggested that Piaget regards language primarily in its phonological aspect. This contrasts with the Chomskian emphasis on syntax. It is further suggested that Piaget's cognitive structures are the psychological counterparts to Chomsky's linguistic notion of a semantically interpreted syntactic marker. The implication in Piaget that semantic and syntactic organization are not independently specifiable is considered plausible. However, Piaget is criticized for ignoring the syntactic problems here.'

'The nature of the intrinsic structure of the child at the onset of language acquisition is a principal area of disagreement between

Chomskians and Piagetians. Chomskian psycholinguists argue that the intrinsic structure of the child is highly specific, in order to account for the discrepancy between the linguistic input and the output of total mastery. This intrinsic structure is characterized by linguistic universals such as the distinction between deep and surface structure and transformational rules. Piagetians argue that the child's intrinsic structure is much more general, the Chomskian specifies being learned in the course of experience'.

PART THREE

Sensorimotor Intelligence

a. Introduction and related studies
b. The concept of object permanence
c. The development of object permanence in animals

a. Introduction and related studies

Introduction

Piaget (1967) considers that the period that extends from birth to the acquisition of language is 'marked by an extraordinary development of the mind.' The importance of this period is sometimes underestimated because 'it is not accompanied by words that permit a step-by-step pursuit of the progress of intelligence and the emotions, as is the case later on'. Piaget emphasizes that this early mental development determines the entire course of psychological evolution. In fact, it is no less than 'a conquest by perception and movement of the entire practical universe that surrounds the small child'.

Piaget cites three stages between birth and the end of the first period: the reflex stage, the stage of the organization of percepts and habits and the stage of sensorimotor intelligence itself. At birth, mental life is limited to 'hereditarily determined sensory and motor coordinations that correspond to instinctual needs, such as intuition'. Piaget stresses that these reflexes are not by any means passive, for from the outset they show genuine activity. Further, they reveal the existence of 'precocious sensorimotor assimilation': for example, the sucking reflexes become refined and improved over time. The sucking reflex also becomes generalized to other sucking activities. 'The infant assimilates a part of his universe to his sucking to the degree that his initial behaviour can be described by saying that for him the world is essentially a thing to be sucked . . . this same universe will also become a thing to be looked at, to listen to, and, as soon as his own movements will allow, to shake.'

This reflex stage soon becomes integrated into habits and organized percepts: the child turns his head in response to a sound, follows a moving object and gradually begins to recognize certain persons as distinct from others. He does not, however, conceptualize a person or even an object. Piaget stresses the essential role of 'circular reactions' at this stage: 'the infant's random movements fortuitously producing something interesting (interesting because it can be assimilated into a prior schema) for him to repeat these new movements immediately' and representing a more advanced form of assimilation.

The third stage, 'which is even more important to the course of development': the stage of practical and sensorimotor intelligence itself. Intelligence actually appears well before language, that is to say, well before internal thought, which presupposes the use of verbal signs (internalized language). It is an entirely practical intelligence based on the manipulation of objects; in place of words and concepts it uses percepts and movements organized into 'action schemata'. Piaget considers that the stage of sensorimotor intelligence leads to the 'construction of an objective universe in which the subject's own body is an element among others and with which the internal life, localized in the subject's own body is contrasted'. (Piaget subdivides these stages even further and gives detailed accounts of each in *The Origin of Intelligence in the Child*, 1953.)

Piaget describes four fundamental processes which characterize the sensorimotor period: the construction of the categories of the object, of space, of causality and of time. He adds the proviso that these refer to purely practical or action categories and not, of course, to ideas or thinking. The elaboration of space is derived from the coordination of movements; causality, the link between an empirical result and some action that has brought it about, and the objectification of time enabling 'the nascent mind' to be extricated 'from its radical unconscious egocentricity' and to be placed in a 'universe'. Piaget (1954) argues with respect to Objects and Space, 'Could it not be said that the object exists in substance from the very beginning, only its localization in space being subject to difficulties? . . . such a distinction is in fact meaningless; to exist as an object is to be ordered in space, for the elaboration of space is precisely the objectification of perceived images', pp. 43–44. An object is conceptually 'permanent' and discrete only insofar as it can be abstracted from its different movements, orientations and locations *vis-à-vis* other objects, from its responses to the child's actions upon it and from the child's own body. The 'object permanence' concept is the hallmark of sensorimotor intelligence and the concept in terms of which the child unites all four aspects into a general picture of the child's conception of the world. Piaget's operational definition of the concept of object permanence involves a comprehension of spatial relations between objects and screens and of the ways in which object-screen relations are modified by the action of the S or of the E. On the other hand, the concept of space is the concept of objects-in-locations, these relations being learnt via the child's own actions on objects.

The development of the concepts of Causality and of Time is 'completely analogous' to that of Objects and Space. Piaget maintains, 'The causal and temporal series . . . constitute merely the other face of the objective and spatial series envisaged hitherto', p. 221. For the child to comprehend 'Causality' he has to conceive of persons and objects as discrete entities, related systematically in a common space. And conversely, the concept of objects and their spatial displacements depends on the child's appreciation of how his actions and those of other persons affect the world. Two types of 'Causality' in sensorimotor intelligence are distinguished: 'Physical Causality' which evolves from an earlier 'phenomenalism' and 'Psychological Causality' which emerges from the infant's sense of his own 'efficacy'. Both involve causal relations and physical contact, both object–object and person–object. The former is defined as 'an objectified and spatial causality affecting the interrelations of things', while the latter as 'a causality . . . uniting intentions with acts'. The infant's concept of Time is what is implied in objects, space and causality. The sensorimotor concept of time is simply the concept of states and events occurring in sequence. It is in terms of an ordered sequence of states and events that the child's memory is organized. Piaget states, '. . . the child remembers the sequential displacements of the objects and sets them in the proper order', (p. 342).

Related studies

Matheny (1975) selected 20 test items from the Bayley Mental Scale (1969), which were equivalent to items used in the Piagetian scales developed by Escalona and Corman (1967) and by Uzgiris and Hunt (1966). These were analyzed for evidence of concordance for samples that included at least 120 identical pairs of twins and 85 same-sex fraternal pairs of twins at ages three, six, nine, and 12 months. Within-pair correlations were computed for the total number of Piagetian-equivalent items passed in the first year. 'Identical twin pairs were found to be consistently more concordant than fraternal twin pairs, the highest levels of significance being found at three and six months, and for items related to prehension, object permanence, and imitation. Within-pair correlations for the total score were .80 for identical pairs and .61 for fraternal pairs; these correlations were significantly different'. The findings substantiated Piaget's assertions regarding the biological origins of sensorimotor capabilities. (Details are given later).

Recently, McCall, Hogarty, and Hurlburt (1972) have carefully studied developmental transitions in infant or sensorimotor intelligence. They correlated factors at the ages of six, 12, 18 and 24 months.

Correlation matrices depicting the factor interrelationships graphically demonstrated a complexity in which convergent, divergent, and parallel complements were present. Since the authors comment that 'the network of transitions between skills at one age and another is likely more specific and complex than once thought,' p. 746, and 'since they were focused on only an 18-month time span, it can be appreciated that the model developed here may prove quite useful for abstracting some degree of order in the changing pattern of ability factors over the life span', Buss and Royce (1975, p. 93).

Conflicting results have been observed from studies measuring infants on sensorimotor scales in relation to social class. Golden and Birns (1968, 1971) reported no difference in sensorimotor performance between lower and middle class infants; however, Hunt (1972), Paraskevopoulos and Hunt (1971) and Wachs, Uzgiris and Hunt (1971) obtained differential performance as a result of social class. Other factors, likewise influence the process of acquisition of sensorimotor behaviours. Uzgiris (1967) proposed that the state of the infant affects how he relates to objects in his environment. 'Certainly, constitutional and health factors play a role. Babies who are apathetic or frequently fretful may not have many optimal periods to explore their milieu. If, in fact, all of these variables might affect sensorimotor development, then it seems necessary to examine how healthy, normally developing infants from a relatively optimal and homogeneous environment progress through sensorimotor stages', Kopp, Sigman, and Parmelee (1974, p. 688).

In a study of ordinality and sensorimotor series, Kopp, Sigman and Parmelee (1973) used Green's (1956) index of consistency to determine ordinality of three subtests of a sensorimotor series. The longitudinal sample of infants were at nine, 12, 15, 18, and 20 months of age. The results demonstrated that scalability could be affected by the responses of infants at different developmental ages. (Details are given later.) In their 1974 study the authors focused on the rate of acquisition of differing sensorimotor behaviours, variability in the performance of such behaviours, and the relationship between performance on the various subtests. The longitudinal performance of 24 healthy full-term infants from middle class homes was evaluated employing an adapted version of the 'Stages of Sensorimotor Intelligence in the Child', devised by Casati and Lézine (1968). Results demonstrated that although there was an overall progression in stage development for the behaviours examined, occasional declines in performance were also evident. Performance on one subtest was generally unrelated to performance on another subtest. The longitudinal data on the development of object permanence compared favourably with previously reported results (King and Seegmiller, 1973;

Koslowski and Bruner, 1972; Miller, Cohen, and Hill, 1970). (Details are given later). In continuation, task characteristics and a stage six sensorimotor problem were studied by Kopp, O'Connor and Finger (1975), who conducted two experiments among 120 children ranging in age from 20 to 34 months. The main problem administered was patterned after Casati and Lézine (1968), with modifications. Results demonstrated that problem solving was enhanced in the transformed condition, with older Ss performing somewhat better than younger Ss. Kopp, O'Connor and Finger suggested that 'cognitive requirements of the problem, as representative of stage six sensorimotor development, remained the same in the original or transformed condition. The modification appeared to permit children to focus their attention on the requirements of the problem, so that a greater number of children demonstrated mental representation'. The authors drew attention to the task characteristics of sensorimotor problems which need to be investigated further. (Details follow).

In Willerman and Fiedler's (1974) study, 'a retrospective check of Boston participants in the Collaborative Perinatal Study identified 100 white children with IQs of 140 or more at four years of age who had been administered the research version of the Bayley Scales of Mental and Motor Development at eight months. The results indicate that this superior group of children were not generally advanced as infants and could not have been distinguished from the total population of infants at eight months. Among these intellectually precocious children, parental education and the child's IQ at four were significantly correlated for boys but not for girls', p. 483.

Nicolich and Raph (1975) were intent to examine the level of symbolic capability as revealed in play, the use of spontaneous vocal imitation and its relationship to symbolic level, and the nature of certain classes of words occurring in spontaneous language. Five female subjects ranging in age from 14 to 19 months were observed monthly in the home for 40-minute periods over a one-year time span. The children were presented with a standard set of toys and engaged in free play and conversation with their mothers. These sessions were videotaped and transcribed. The videotape was divided into play episodes, each of which was judged and assigned a symbolic play level as suggested by Piaget (1962). There were consistent patterns of vocal imitative behaviour and of symbolic development. The use of language to code precursors of operational intelligence was remarkably consistent for all children observed. It was suggested that common cognitive skills developed during the sensorimotor period form the foundation for these patterns of development. (Details are given later).

In a study entitled: 'Play and language: the development of representational thought in infancy', Rosenblatt (1975) focuses on the early relationship between cognition and language, 'in particular, the emergence of conceptual abilities which mark the transition from "sensorimotor" and "representational" thought'. Twenty infants were studied with respect to toy play strategies, language acquisition and other representational skills (imitation, categorization, seriation, and object permanence), 20 simple sensorimotor and 100 symbolic play behaviours were time-sampled at monthly intervals between 9 and 18 months and again at 24 months. A mother—infant play session was observed at 3 monthly intervals from 9 to 18 months and at 24 months. Measures of play behaviour significantly correlated with language development, 'such that children who have early symbolic play also show faster word acquisition and a wider range of referents and word types'. Early talkers achieve object permanence earlier and are more advanced with respect to sorting strategies. Maternal speech correlated with child language. Results therefore suggested that 'early language . . . is part of the development of a general referential system which bridges sensorimotor and representational thought. The ability to select and order responses, and to apply differentiated and appropriate responses to objects precedes, and then parallels the selection of categories and meanings in the first set of words'. (Further details follow).

The relationship between the cognitive and linguistic pluralization rules in 18 38-month-old children was studied by Coffman (1975) in 32 infants. Subjects were scored for operativity on a cognitive task in which utilization of plural cues was necessary for success, and a linguistic task which evaluated their use of plural markings in the production and comprehension modes. The three youngest age groups had significantly higher scores in the cognitive than the linguistic task. Coffman interpreted the results as offering firm substantiation for the Piagetian hypothesis that language is built on broader intellectual schemas and is not an innately programmed function. (Details follow).

In a study entitled, 'Sensory-motor intelligence and semantic relations in early child grammar', Edwards (1973) elaborated a system of semantic clause-types for the description of the relational meanings 'that are apparently expressed universally in the two-word speech of young children. These semantic relations are compared to the concepts invoked in Piaget's descriptions of sensorimotor intelligence, in particular to the concepts of permanent objects and their spatial relations, to the dual concepts of persons as physical objects and as active beings, and to the role of persons as causers of changes in the locativity of objects. A close correspondence is found, and it is claimed that the nature of sensorimotor intelligence severely constrains the range of relational meanings expressed, including even the child's notions of possessive relations between persons and objects, of attributes of objects, and his use of apparently "experiential" verbs'.

Daehler and Bukatko (1974) administered a series of five two-choice discrimination-learning tasks to a sample of 48 two-year-old children. 'For some children the positive instance on each problem belonged to a common category, while for others no conceptual relationship existed among the stimuli on succeeding problems. Ss committed remarkably few errors, averaging only slightly over one error per problem. Children over 30 months of age did better than younger children, and girls learned faster than boys after the first problem. Presence of a category relationship among positive instances was not significantly related to learning, perhaps because discriminations could be acquired so rapidly', p. 378.

To extend Piaget's thoughts on sensorimotor development to the pre-operational child's performance of a Piagetian rate-time task, Longobardi and Wolff (1973) examined specifically, 'the ability to imitate motorically the experimenter's performance of the task . . . compared with the ability to give conceptually correct verbal replies to questions about the task'. Second grade children were able to imitate a given rate-time relationship whereas their verbal (symbolic) conceptualization remained as inadequate as that of nursery children, who were unable to imitate these relationships. 'The differential development of rate-time relationships in the two response modes suggests the need for, in Piaget's terms, "a logic of coordination of actions" which may exist in the absence of any indication of the symbolic understanding of logical or infralogical relations in the child.'

Bryant (1974) casts doubt on the Mounoud and Bower (1975) study. The latter authors studied children's judgments of weight by measuring the amount of pressure exerted on each weight when the child gripped it. 'They also worked with one quantity at a time. They found convincing evidence that the young child understands that perceptually transforming something does not alter its weight. Children as young as eighteen months did not alter the pressure with which they gripped an object after they saw it transformed. The study is a neat one, but Mounoud and Bower's conclusions from it are questionable. They argue that there are two levels in the understanding of invariance, one behavioural and the other conceptual. They suggest that their experiment taps the first of these, showing that the very young child can organize his behaviour around the assumption of invariance without being able to deal with the principle on a conceptual level. They agree with Piaget that his experiments demonstrate children's inability to understand the invariance of weight at a conceptual level before the age of ten. They do not define these two levels very precisely and admit that the connections between them are not yet clear. Perhaps the reason for this obscurity is that the behavioural—conceptual split does not really exist, and that the real difference between their procedure and that of Piaget was that theirs involved only one quantity and was the purer test, while Piaget's involved two quantities with all the consequent ambiguity. The difference between the two experiments is probably one of design and controls, and there are no real grounds for thinking that one experiment is more representative of a certain level of behaviour in real life than the other', p. 176. (Mounoud and Bower abstract appears later).

Further studies relating to the sensorimotor stage as a whole are reported in Modgil (1974).

b. The concept of object permanence

Introduction

The formation of the scheme of the permanent object is closely related to the whole spatio-temporal and causal organization of the practical universe. The six stages as postulated by Piaget (1954) of the development of the object concept correspond to those of intellectual development in general. Piaget summarizes the stages as follows: 'During the first two stages . . . The infantile universe is formed of pictures that can be recognized but that have no substantial permanence or spatial organization'. 'During the third stage . . . a beginning of permanence is conferred on things by prolongation of the movements of accommodation . . . but no systematic search for absent objects . . . During the fourth stage . . . there is searching for objects that have disappeared but no regard for their displacements . . . During a fifth stage . . . the object is constituted to the extent that it is permanent individual substance and inserted in the groups of displacements, but the child still cannot take account of changes of position brought about outside the field of direct perception. In a sixth stage (beginning at the age of 16 to 18 months) there is an image of absent objects and their displacements.'

During the first four or five months (Stages I and II), Piaget observes that the infant can follow moving objects visually, moving his head and eyes so that the object may be kept in view. However the infant loses interest as soon as the object is out of sight. Piaget argues that the infant is simply involved in a 'circular reaction' such that a return to his original position brings the earlier sight back into existence. There are no grounds to assume that the infant is responding to objects as independent entities in the world. Such an interpretation would involve 'a most improbable power of spatial representation and intellectual construction', Piaget, 1954, p. 12.

During Stage III (roughly three—eight months of age) Piaget found that the infant learns to grasp objects which are first located visually. When such objects are covered by a cloth, he acts as though the object has gone out of existence — the object has reality only as long as it is in view. Piaget recorded the following instance:

'At 0:8 (15) (age eight months and 15 days) Lucienne is seated and tries to recapture a celluloid stork (containing a rattle) which she had just held and shaken . . . I place the stork beside her right knee, covering it with the edge of the cloth on which she is seated; nothing would be simpler than to find it again. Moreover, Lucienne has watched each of my movements most attentively and they were slow and clearly visible. However, as soon as the stork disappears under the cloth, Lucienne stops looking at it and looks at my hand. She examines it with great interest but pays no more attention to the cloth', Piaget, 1937 (1954), p. 38.

Piaget (1947) comments on observations such as these, 'He thus behaves as though the object were absorbed by the cloth and ceased to exist at the very moment that it left the perceptual field; or else, and this amounts to the same thing, he possesses no behaviour enabling him to search for the object which has disappeared — whether by action (lifting the screen) or by thought (imaging)'.

At about 9.5 months, Stage IV, the infant develops the ability to remove the cloth from the hidden object and actively search for the object which has disappeared. Piaget asserts that during the early months, prior to the infant's ability to grasp and handle objects, the surrounding environment must be like a series of pictures (*tableaux*) that have no order or stability. Things which surround him are not three-dimensional objects in space, but rather as impressions which are either two-dimensional or as perceptual conglomerates (*faisceaux*) that are mixtures of what may be termed 'subjective impressions' and the sensations that come from the world. Activity plays a vital role in effecting the transition from passive perceptual impressions to an ordered and coherent universe.

At 12 months, Stage V, the infant has mastered the task of finding objects that are hidden successively in different positions, even when this demands an active search for the object. However, difficulties may arise with complicated situations. At approximately 18 months the infant is no longer misled by manipulations and will preserve the permanence of the object.

The main criterion in Piaget's stage six is the child's ability to return to and search for an object after a distraction, during which the object has been covered.

Related studies

Bower (1967) has, in part, criticized Piaget's concept of object permanence. Through a series of ingenious experiments, Bower has published convincing evidence which suggests that two- to three-month-old infants have a perceptual version of the concept of object permanence. Bower is in agreement with Piaget in finding that if an object disappears in an abrupt, discontinuous manner, the infant acts as if it no longer existed for him. However, if it disappears gradually and continuously, the infant behaves for a short period as though it were still present or would reappear. Bower concludes that 'these primitive, perception-based discriminations regarding permanence and impermanence are later subordinated to conceptual rules to the concept of object permanence. Unlike the three-month-old, the 12-month-old has come to believe in the continued existence of certain objects (e.g. his mother), regardless of the psychophysical properties of their disappearance — even when his lower order, perceptual operations have given him a verdict of out-of-existence rather than out-of-sight'. More recently, Bower and Paterson (1972), after supporting the hypothesis 'that there is an object concept developing from birth onwards and that facilitatory intervention at one point will speed development at later points', draw attention to the need to devise a theory to link the various stages of the development of the object concept. 'While Bower has questioned this view of the infant's world, his very interesting studies are still too sketchy to offer an alternative conception for the behavioural phenomena described by Piaget and replicated by others', Uzgiris (1973, p. 183).

Piaget (1954) reported that if one presents a six—eight-month-old infant with a toy that is then covered (with a cloth) before the infant can grasp it, the S will make no attempt to remove the cover to obtain the toy. The interpretation is that an object that is no longer visible no longer exists. However, Bower, Broughton and Moore (1971) demonstrated that infants below the age of 20 weeks did not know that a moving object can stop and become stationary. The authors argued that when such infants were presented with a moving object that stopped, the infants thought the stationary object was a new object. Focusing on Bower's *et al.* methodology and explanations, Bower and Paterson (1973) assert that 'it could be argued that the infants who show such continuation of tracking do so because they are simply unable to arrest an ongoing head and eye movement. Alternatively, one could argue that infants have learned that an event on one side of a screen is usually followed by an event on the other side of the screen; when one event, movement toward the screen, stops, the infants look over for the other event, movement away from the screen', p. 161. They therefore studied the separation of place, movement, and object in the world of the infant and reported that infants less than 16 weeks of age continued to track a moving object after they had seen it stop. 'They will look for an object in a familiar place, even if they see it go elsewhere. These errors reflect a low order concept of the object, one which does not include place and movement in a differentiated way', p. 161. (Details are given later.)

Bower and Paterson (1974) argue that there are problems in debating 'a topic such as the development of the object concept, since the measures used to assess the status of the object concept change drastically during the alleged period of development, and the concept itself does not seem to develop in any continuous fashion. An acceleration experiment is performed to discover whether or not intervention at one point of the hypothetical process effects development at later points. The results are positive, suggesting that there is, indeed, an object concept that develops over an 18-month period. An unexpected result of the study was the finding that development is discontinuous and stage-like, rather than continuous', p. 47.

Bower and Paterson (1973, *op. cit.*) reported that until five months, infants continue to track along a familiar trajectory even if the object stops midway. These tracking errors are identical to those reported by Harris (1974) for manual search in that the infant orients toward both the new and the old location. 'Thus Bower and Paterson (1973) note that the infant orients momentarily towards the stationary object and then continues tracking along the familiar trajectory. They ascribe such errors to an inability to identify the stationary object with the moving object. However, why should such errors then reappear in manual search? Presumably, a conceptual insight, such as the ability to identify stationary and moving objects, should be transferable to a different motor system. An alternative interpretation is that such tracking errors are "growth" errors resulting from the acquisition of a new tracking strategy: extrapolating along a trajectory in order to recover a fast-moving object or an object which moves behind a screen. Bower (1972) has reported some data supporting this interpretation; very young infants who could not extrapolate a trajectory did not exhibit the tracking errors . . .', Harris, 1974, p. 541.

Relating to perseverative errors, Harris (1973) suggested an alternative interpretation to that advanced by Piaget (1954). The former author reported that 10-month-old infants were able to search correctly in a new place, but that perseverative errors were possible if a delay was introduced between disappearance and the opportunity to search, or of cues previously associated with finding the object distracted the infant after its disappearance at a new place. 'A hypothesis of proactive interference in short-term memory was proposed to account for the finding that the infant could search correctly but was vulnerable to interference', Harris (1974, p. 535). In his 1974 study therefore, Harris studied perseverative search at a visibly empty place via two experiments in 40 infants. Results demonstrated that when an object moved to a new place, year-old Ss approached both its new location and its prior location. The infants did not treat these object locations as mutually exclusive even when the object was visible at the new location and visibly absent from the old location. Harris concluded that perseverative errors were not simply a memory problem and puts forward possible explanations. (Details appear later). (See also Harris, 1975).

That perseverative errors sometimes occurred even when transparent covers were used so that the object remained visible at a new location were reported by Butterworth (1973). However, Harris (1974) argues that, 'This finding raises difficulties for the memory hypothesis. Perseverative errors cannot be attributed to proactive interference in storage since the infant is not required to remember where the object is if it is visible. The hypothesis might regain plausibility if it could be shown that for the infant, the object although not hidden, has effectively disappeared from view. For example the infant might look away from the object before searching. If, on the other hand, the infant demonstrates that he knows the whereabouts of the object, but still perseverates, this would suggest that Piaget may be correct in arguing that perserverative errors reveal the infant's conceptual naivete about objects', pp. 535—536.

The effects of motor skill on object permanence was studied by Bower and Wishart (1972). The authors maintain that, 'Piaget found that infants in the first year of life will not remove a cloth or a cup that they have seen cover a toy. Part of the difficulty is a motor skill problem. However, deficits in motor skill are not sufficient to account for the failure in the situation. We cannot assume that out of sight is out of mind for such infants for they will reach out to obtain an object that has been made to go out of sight by switching off the rooms lights, leaving the baby in total darkness', p. 165. (Details appear later). The findings of Gottfried and Brody (1975) (discussed fully in Volume Four: *School Curriculum and Test Development*, in the present series, *Piagetian Research*) lent credence and elaborate the findings by Bower and Wishart and Kopp (1973). Bower and Wishart found that motor ability played an important role in passing on particular object permanence item and Kopp found that fine motor prehension was associated with the type of schemas elicited toward objects. Gottfried and Brody while supporting these contentions indicated 'that an infant who was motorically precocious was likely to exhibit patterns of behaviour which were representative of more advanced schemas or levels of sensorimotor development. Furthermore, motor development yielded a similar correlational network to that of the sensorimotor scales. For the most part, the variables that correlated with sensorimotor development also correlated with motor development to a similar degree', (*ibid.,* p. 384).

Bryant (1974) has argued, 'According to Piaget the fact that babies as young as this do not reach out and search for objects which they have seen being put behind some cover or other demonstrates that they think that once the object disappears from view it ceases to exist. This may be so: but our discovery of cross-modal recognition in groups of babies whose mean ages were always less than nine months shows that at least in some situations babies do have a mechanism which could tell them that an object which has disappeared still goes on existing. Suppose that a baby looks at an object which is in his hand and then moves his hand so that, although he is still holding the object, he can no longer see it. If now he can recognize the shape which he holds as equivalent to the shape which he saw before it disappeared, he has an effective way of understanding that the object still exists, despite the fact that he can no longer see it', p. 165.

In a study by Brown (1973) a group of infants who had failed a standard object-permanence test were shown a desirable object that was then hidden by a screen. All of the infants were able to remove the screen to obtain the object, although in a subsequent test, all failed even to attempt to remove a cup that was covering an object. Bower (1974) comments that it is the nature of the transition to 'out of sight' rather than the mere fact of being out of sight that appears to be important. The implication is 'that the infant cannot succeed in the standard object-permanence tests until he comprehends the relation "inside". He must reformulate his rule, "Two objects cannot be in the same place at the same time," to read, "Two objects cannot be in the same place at the same time unless one is inside the other".' (Further discussion appears in Bower, 1974, pp. 209–11).

The enhancement of hidden object search in six-month-old infants presented with a continuously sounding hidden object was studied by Ginsburg and Wong (1973). The study involved eight six-month-old infants who showed no ability to search for a variety of nonsounding hidden objects. During phase one, each S was presented with a nonsounding Plexiglas music box which was removed from his grasp and gradually covered with a white cloth. Phase two was similar to phase one except that the music box sounded continuously from the time just before presentation to the infant until after the object was completely concealed. Phase three was identical to phase one and all phases comprised of three trials. Response differences between sounding and nonsounding trials were significant (sign. test, p = .016, one-tailed). Results were considered 'in the context of the possible orientating effect produced by the continuous auditory signal of the object's presence which served to maintain the infant's attention throughout the entire concealment procedure', p. 142. (Details are given later).

Smillie (1972) critically examined Piaget's theory of the construction of the object in infancy. 'It is found that his notion of "perceptual tableaux", used to describe the experience of the young infant, is contradicted by the evidence of Bower's experiments. Reinterpreting Piaget's evidence, support is found for an initial period of visual realism followed by a period in which the infant explores the possibilities of his own actions. Following these substages the infant coordinates the information obtained from vision and manipulation. This interpretation involves a shift of emphasis rather than a total rejection of Piaget's theory', p. 171. (Details of the study are given later).

The development of the concept of object was studied by Uzgiris (1973) employing the scale of Visual Pursuit and the Permanence of Objects constructed by Uzgiris and Hunt (1966), which comprises a sequence of 14 steps marking progress in the development of the object concept rather than the six levels described as stages by Piaget. Achievements in other branches of psychological development were also examined in the infants using such scales as (a) the Development of Means for Obtaining Desired Environmental Events Scale; (b) the Construction of Object Relations in Space Scale and (c) the Operational Causality Scale. The Ss were 12 infants, six girls and six boys who were observed in their own homes. Uzgiris concludes, '. . . an examination of the relationships between achievements pertaining to object concept development and achievements in three other branches of psychological functioning suggests four distinct levels in object concept development. The first appears to parallel Piaget's stage three and seems to reflect a minimal level of ability to incorporate perceptually absent objects or events into ongoing schemes of action. The second level appears to span stages four and five in Piaget's system and seems to reflect an increasing differentiation of objects from the actions in which they are incorporated, which entails substantiation of objects and contributes to the use of objects as means for achieving desired goals. The third level appears to coincide with the beginning of Piaget's stage six, evidenced by search for an object hidden by means of an invisible displacement, and seems to be achieved subsequent to considerable exploration of the relationships between objects in space. This level probably reflects the articulation of a matrix of spatial relations in which displacements of objects may be envisioned and which makes possible the exploitation of perceived relations between objects for achieving desired goals. The final level coincides with the culmination of the sensorimotor period and reflects the achievement of the ability to represent the displacement of independently moving objects within a spatial framework', p. 200. (Details follow.)

To investigate Piaget's theory of object concept development, Kramer, Hill and Cohen (1975) administered a series of six tasks in a combined longitudinal/cross-sectional design incorporating a number of methodological controls. 'The tasks spanned the entire sensorimotor period and included single versus sequential displacements combined with visible or invisible hidings. Thirty-six infants from five to 32 months of age at initial testing were drawn equally from day-care and home settings. All infants received the six tasks during each of three testing sessions over a six-month period. Clear evidence was obtained for task ordinality as proposed by Piaget, with ordinality coefficients ranging from .71 to .82 for the three testing sessions. Performance changes across the three sessions were also ordinal in 80 per cent of the cases. Expected age, task, and session effects and accompanying interactions were also obtained', p. 149. (Details appear later.)

Bower (1974) emphasized the importance of repetition: reviewing studies that indicate that the first phase of a concept or skill is necessary for the mature expression of that concept or skill he speculated that support can be given to Piaget and others who have shown there are almost no mature concepts that do not have a behavioural expression in infancy. 'The theoretical consequences of taking repetitive phenomena seriously are equally great. For example it seems profitless to study the development of conservation as something occurring between 5 years and 9 years of age, if this phase of the development is entirely specified by development occurring in infancy'.

The deficiencies of the young infant's size concept is shown in a simple, ingenious experiment performed by Greenfield, Nelson and Saltzman (1972). Infants of one year were shown a set of 'nesting' objects and were shown how to construct a 'nested' structure. All of the infants made some attempt at stacking but were unable to organize the objects according to their size. The infants were able to perceive the size of the objects relative to their own hands as demonstrated by the ability to pick up the objects successfully. It can be concluded that 'size' at this stage can be said to be relative to the infant, not a relation between objects.

Bell (1970) showed that infants tended to be more advanced in the concept of persons than in the concept of inanimate objects as permanent. Furthermore, individual differences in the rate of development of person permanence were related to the quality of attachment that an infant showed towards his mother. In turn, this affected the development of object permanence. She concluded 'the quality of a baby's interaction with his mother is one of the crucial dimensions of "environmental influence" to affect this type of sensorimotor development'. (Details are given in Modgil, 1974, pp. 23–24).

Golden and Birns (1971) examined infants between 18 and 24 months of age from different SES groups on the Cattell and Piaget object scales. The authors concluded that social class differences in cognitive development were not evident during the sensorimotor period; further, that SES differences emerge from CA 18 to CA 36 months when language develops. (Details are given in Modgil, 1974, p. 25). Babska (1965) has extended the research beyond the sensorimotor stage six. She considers that the object concept is not fully operative until about three years of age — a research area termed by Flavell

Stage IV marks an important transition. Before Stage IV, the infant lacks object permanence and knows an object and its location only in the context of his ongoing actions: he cannot find hidden things or can only find them if he has begun to reach for them before they disappear. In Stage IV, the infant is aware of object permanence: when he observes an object disappear, he searches for it even when he has not begun to reach for it before its disappearance. In Piaget's experiments an object is hidden in one place (A) and then in a second place (B). After the infant finds the object at A, he watches the object being hidden at B. However, when the object disappears from view, the infant searches at A. This establishes the pattern of success at A and failure at B and is referred to as 'AB'.

Of the follow-up studies, the majority have demonstrated that the task of finding an object hidden only at 'A' (object in one place' is relatively easier than the task of finding an object hidden both at 'A' and 'B' ('B' refers to the object transferred to a second place). Such studies include those of Decarie (1965), Bell (1968), Escalona and Corman (1967), Miller, Cohen and Hill (1969) and Smith (1970). The study by Miller, Cohen and Hill on object permanence involved two types of administration. The replication sample was given object permanence tasks in rank order of difficulty, whereas in the extension condition the task was randomized. Kopp, Sigman and Parmelee's (1974) administration of the test was comparable to the replication condition. The scores of the infants in the Kopp, Sigman and Parmelee sample on the search for hidden object subtest were transformed to correspond to the Miller *et al.* procedure. The resultant patterns were quite similar, although, at the older ages, the Kopp *et al.* sample indicated scores closer to the Miller *et al.* replication condition than to the extension condition.

These studies, however, did not provide convincing evidence as to whether unsuccessful behaviour at 'B' is followed by exploration at 'A', or termination of the search. Furthermore, the universality and age-relatedness of such a phenomenon is uncertain. For example, only two of 25 eight-and-half-month-old infants in Bell's study (1968), who searched successfully at 'A', failed at 'B'. However, it was not made clear whether either of the two infants failed 'B' by searching at 'A' or simply terminated the search. Other studies, e.g. Appel and Gratch (1969), Bower (1967), and Charlesworth (1966), who also examined the development of object-permanence, recorded their observations in a one-position situation only. Of particular interest is Charlesworth's study, in which a 'trick condition' was introduced involving a small foot-operated 'trap door' in the tray of the child's high chair. This enabled a 'more sensitive measure of a child's cognitive progress' (see Flavell, 1971).

Gratch and Landers' investigation (1967) concluded that 'the visual orientation of infants during the delay between hiding and searching was related to their successful searching behaviour in the AB experimental paradigm' (i.e. a pattern of success at A and failure at B). In continuation, Landers' study (1971) involved infants 'playing a two-position hidden-object game. Infants who had much experience of reaching and finding an object at the "A" position made longer error runs at this position than infants who had little searching experience at "A" or infants who had much experience just observing objects hidden at "A" but no experience searching for them'. (The study is discussed in Modgil, 1974, pp. 27–28). In an attempt partly to replicate and partly to extend Landers' study, Gratch and Landers (1971) generally confirmed Piaget's (1954) Stage IV in the development of object concepts using a longitudinal procedure and a short time delay (three seconds) and replicated Piaget's Stage IV findings in most of their Ss over several biweekly sessions. As in many such tasks with young children, there was little evidence of learning over trials, but there was improvement between sessions. The study produced evidence that suggested the mechanisms of transition from looking for an object where it had been to looking where it was last seen. Gratch and Landers also observed that failure to encode the information from the displacement, which would be suggested by Piaget, seems to occur only in young Stage IV children. Older children in Stage IV appeared to be in conflict over where to search and decide in favour of the initial (and incorrect) location after some vacillation. (The study is described in Modgil, 1974, pp. 26–27).

Luria (1959) reported a phenomenon similar to Piaget's Stage IV behaviour in 16- to 18-month-old children. 'When the object was hidden several times in one location and then hidden in another, many of the children would reach toward the old location but search for the object in the new. With a 10-second delay imposed between hiding and the child's search, most of the children could still find the object when it was hidden in the first location. However, when the object was hidden in a second location in the delay condition, the majority of children returned to the initial location even though they had clearly observed the object being placed in the new container. Children in the 20—24 month age range in Luria's study solved this problem. Luria interprets these findings as showing that the directive function of the visual trace loses its effectiveness over the 10-second delay in the younger children. . . . it is interesting that Luria never states that the child forgets where the object was hidden but attributes the errors to stereotyped response patterns', Webb, Massar, and Nadolny, 1972, p. 92. These authors examined information and strategy in the young child's search for hidden objects. Children aged 16- and 14-months were studied in three choice delayed-reaction problems. 'Sixteen-month-olds were able to locate a hidden object correctly on initial trials but made subsequent errors due to a tendency to return to a previous location. The majority of these children, however, located the object correctly with their second choice. 14-month-olds were less successful. These data indicate that the information from the hiding remained effective even while the child was making his initial error', p. 91. The authors interpreted the findings in terms of search strategy and memory. (Details are given later).

Evans and Gratch (1972) evaluated Piaget's explanation of the $A\bar{B}$ error: 'twelve 9-month-old infants found a toy twice in succession at A and then observed that a different toy was hidden at B. 12 infants saw the same toy hidden at both A and B. The majority of the infants in each group made the AB error, suggesting that the $A\bar{B}$ error may be best viewed as simply a place-going error', p. 682. (Details appear in Modgil, 1974, pp. 29—30).

A direct empirical relation exists between children's object labelling and their performance on object permanence tasks (Roberts and Black, 1972) and the findings of LeCompte and Gratch (1972) in which infants' object concepts were verified by a sensitive 'trick' method in which the E would on some trials trick the S by surreptitiously substituting a different object from the one hidden for the child to discover. Eighteen months old infants demonstrated 'high puzzlement' and carried on searching for the missing toy. The Ss had a clear idea of a particular missing toy and therefore a nameable one, rather than merely an object or merely a place in which to look. Piaget's contentions concerning the development of the object concept were upheld. (The study is described in Modgil, 1974, p. 30).

Gratch, Appel, Evans, LeCompte, and Wright (1974) maintain that Piaget explains the Stage IV error as a failure to assimilate the new place of hiding rather than a forgetting of it. Further, that Piaget's hypothesis predicts that the probability of error should not vary with the length of the delay interval. 'Nine-month-old infants were delayed 0, one, three, or seven sec. before having the opportunity to search. Infants in all conditions, save 0 sec, were likely to err. While Piaget's hypothesis was not supported by the results of the 0-sec condition, subsequent analyses of the data provided some support for Piaget's hypothesis', p. 71. (Details are given later).

c. *The development of object permanence in animals*

Gruber, Girgus and Banuazizi (1971) and Vaughter, Smotherman, and Ordy (1972) administered tests of object permanence to kittens and young squirrel monkeys. The former observed that object permanence in the cat emerged in a sequence similar to the one described by Piaget for the child. However, the sequence was completed more rapidly (at 16 to 24 weeks of age) in the cat and culminated in less complex object-related behaviours. Vaughter *et al.* studied object permanence in the squirrel monkey and observed behaviours that Piaget described as characteristic of varied stages in the development of object permanence in the infant. Young squirrel monkeys of various ages demonstrated differential performance on object permanence tasks with the oldest Ss performing at the higher levels. (Both studies are described below). Likewise, the development of object permanence was studied by Wise, Wise, and Zimmerman (1974) in a longitudinal study of two infant rhesus monkeys in a human analogue testing situation and two sub-human analogue testing situations. (See below).

In order to study the development of object permanence in the cat, Gruber, Girgus and Banuazizi (*op. cit.*) modified Piaget's methods of investigating object permanence in children. This modification helped the authors form eight behavioural tests. 'In a study of laboratory-reared animals, it was found that cats reach an early developmental limit. Unlike children, they are unable to follow an object through a series of invisible displacements. House-reared cats showed similar limitations, but advanced more rapidly than cage-reared animals. A longitudinal study suggests that cats go through four stages rather than the six found by Piaget in children. In the first 24 weeks of life, kittens develop as far as children do in their first year, but the child's behaviour with respect to vanished objects eventually becomes more complex and more general', p. 9. (Fuller details are given later).

The development of object permanence in the infant squirrel monkey was studied by Vaughter, Smotherman, and Ordy (*op. cit.*) as it related to response training in a Wisconsin General Test Apparatus. Two behavioural tests, patterned after Piaget, were adapted for monkeys: an object-permanence task and an object-overpermanence task. Results showed that the typical Wisconsin General Test Apparatus response-training procedures assume that the S, from the outset, has a fully developed object concept: 'the object concept develops in the infant squirrel monkey: and the development of object concept permanence in the infant squirrel monkey generally follows along the sequence described by Piaget', p. 34. (Details follow).

Wise, Wise and Zimmerman (*op. cit.*) examined the development of object permanence 'in a longitudinal study of two infant rhesus monkeys in a human analogue testing situation and two sub-human analogue testing situations. The ages at which certain object-related behaviours were demonstrated by the subjects as stable responses were found by the presentation of tasks that involved various manipulations of objects. In each testing situation was found a sequence of development of object permanence that was very similar to the one described by Piaget for the child, and in each case the sequence culminated in behaviours nearly as complex as those described by Piaget for the two-year-old human infant', p. 429. (Details are given later).

Abstracts

Stages in the development of the object concept
T.G.R. Bower and J.G. Paterson, 1972

AIM / An examination of the stages in the development of the object concept.

SUBJECTS / N = 66. The infants were assigned to either a control and an experimental group and equated for birth order, sex and parental occupation.

METHOD / The tracking task was patterned after Bower and Paterson (1973). 'The object to be tracked was a 10cm diameter bullseye ... It was mounted at the end of an arm 30cm in length, driven by a sweep generator at .24 cycles per sec., through an arc of 180 degrees. The infant sat one meter from the display ... Head and eye movements were monitored by a TV camera ... The presentation "began" when the infant first looked at the display ... The experimental group was given weekly exposure to the tracking task from 12 weeks until 16 weeks. The control group was given an equivalent number of laboratory visits that did not involve tracking and then tested on tracking at 16 weeks . . . An object was covered by a cloth in view of the infant. If the infant succeeded in obtaining the object, the stage four-five transition testing was begun. Two cloths were placed on the table, and the object hidden under one of them, A. After retrieval and recovery from the infant, it was again hidden under the same cloth, A. After retrieval and recovery from the infant, it was hidden under the other cloth, B. After this, new cloths and a new toy were introduced, and the procedure repeated. After each AAB sequence toys and cloths were changed. The side chosen as the A side varied randomly from trial block to trial block. Six AAB sequences were run through. When the child reached the criterion of six errorless B trials, the stage five-six testing sequence was begun. On each week thereafter the infant was given one AAB trial, as described above, before the testing proper began. The testing procedure was as follows. Two cloths were placed on the table. An object was placed under one cloth, with the baby watching. The positions of the two cloths were then transposed. Six trials were given', p. 51.

RESULTS / The results demonstrated that an object concept developed over the 18-month period studied, and that facilitatory intervention at one point will accelerate development at later points. Further, that the development was discontinuous and stage-like. The results and related problems are discussed in relation to Bower's (1967, 1971) investigations.

The separation of place, movement, and object in the world of the infant
T.G.R. Bower and J.G. Paterson, 1973
First Study
AIM / The authors argue, 'If the presence of a screen is the cause of the continuation of tracking behaviour, the behaviour should not appear in the absence of a screen. If, on the other hand, the Bower, Broughton and Moore (1971) hypothesis is valid, continuation of tracking should be as likely in the absence of a screen as in the presence of a screen'. The first experiment was undertaken to decide between these two hypotheses.

SUBJECTS / N = 48, with an age-range of 12 to 23 weeks.

METHOD / 'The object to be tracked was a 10cm diameter bullseye . . . It was mounted at the end of an arm 30cm in length, driven by a sweep generator at .24 cycles per second, through an arc of 180 degrees. The infant sat one meter from the display . . . Head and eye movements were monitored by a TV camera mounted behind the display . . . The object was set in motion before the infant was brought in. The presentation began when the infant first looked at the display . . . 20 movement cycles were presented. The last cycle and a random three others incorporated a stop, in which the object stopped moving for 10 sec. Stops were always made in the central 90 degrees of the arc. Records were scored for frequency of tracking on all trials', p. 162.

RESULTS / The results 'serve to eliminate both of the alternative hypotheses'. The continuation of tracking was noted 'at the same ages as before, despite the absence of a screen. The frequency of the behaviour declined with age ($r = -.65$, $p < 01$)', p. 163. Moreover, all the infants were able to stop, when the object stopped. It was only after making the stop that the infants continued tracking.

Second Study

AIM / The authors maintain, 'If it is true that infants do not realize that a moving object is the same object when it becomes stationary, it should also be true that the same infants would not realize that a stationary object is the same object once it starts to move. Just as the first belief results in tracking errors, so should the second', p. 163. The second experiment was conducted to test this contention.

SUBJECTS / N = 60. Twenty infants at each age levels 11, 16 and 21 weeks respectively. Half the Ss were assigned to procedure A, and half to B.

METHOD / 'The mobile object . . . was an electronically controlled carrier, 6 x 2 x 2cm., mounted on a 1 meter rail. On it were mounted three lights which flashed in synchrony at a rate of .6Hz. The speed of movement of the carrier was 8cm per sec. It moved between three defined positions, the centre of the rail, C, and the two ends, R and L . . . Eye movements were recorded by means of two TV cameras, aligned with the infant and position R, in one case, and with the infant and position L in the other . . .'. In procedure A infant sat opposite position C. '. . . Five seconds after the infant had been sat down the object moved, to L for half the Ss, to R for the other half. The sequence continued thus: C – R – C – R – C – R – C – R – C – **L** – C // pause = 10 secs. // – L – C – L – C – L – C – L – C – **R** – Each sequence thus comprised four cycles of movement in one direction, followed by a catch trial where the object moved in the opposite direction, followed by four cycles of movement in that direction, followed by another catch trial. Time at a position was five sec.; transit time was five sec. Eye movements were scored by observers from the videotape. Since the cameras were conjugate with two positions and the infant, the judgment could be made with great accuracy (Gibson and Danielson, 1963)', p. 166.

Procedure B was similar to procedure A except that 'the carrier moved over the centre position of the track, using a distance equal to that from centre to L or R in procedure A', p. 167.

RESULTS / The authors conclude that all subjects were able to track the object on the noncatch trials. 'There were only eight failing trials, and these were evenly spread across all three groups. The situation with the catch trials was quite different. There, the predicted errors did occur, with both procedures although less with B than A', p. 167.

The effects of motor skills on object permanence
T.G.R. Bower and J.G. Wishart, 1972

Experiment One

AIM / A replication of the results reported by Bower (1967) was undertaken.

SUBJECTS / N = 16 aged 21 months.

METHOD / The materials consisted of a stylized manikin toy, a transparent occluder plastic cup, and the opaque occluder was a white plastic cup. The toy was placed within reach of the infants and their free capture time noted. The toy was withdrawn after 15 seconds. 'In its original location was placed one of the occluders, the opaque to eight babies, the transparent to the remainder. Free capture time was recorded. The occluder was then taken away and the toy replaced in its original location. Before the baby could take the toy again the opaque occluder was placed over the toy. The baby was then given three minutes to remove the occluder before the trial was terminated. At the end of the trial the occluder was removed revealing the object which the infant was allowed to pick up and retain for 15 seconds. At the end of this time the toy was removed and replaced in its original location, this time being covered by the transparent occluder. Trial duration was again three minutes, save that if an infant had a hand on the occluder at the end of three minutes he was given a further two minutes to complete his response . . . if the infant had the toy, it was taken away, replaced and recovered by the opaque occluder, with a trial duration equal to that given with the transparent occluder. If the infant did not have the toy at the end of the transparent occluder trial, the occluder was removed, and the infant allowed to take and retain the toy for 15 seconds before the second opaque occluder trial was begun', p. 168.

RESULTS / That there is no difference between an opaque and a transparent occluder as obstacles in a manual search task was rejected. However, it was not concluded that the transparent occluder offered no difficulties.

Experiment Two

AIM / 'If out of sight is out of mind for the hand the absence of behavioural problems will not help the infant. If, on the other hand, out of sight is simply a problem, then the absence of the additional behavioural problems posed by the classic situation might allow the babies to succeed'.

SUBJECTS / N = 12 aged 20 weeks.

METHOD / The Piagetian object permanence test administered was similar to the one as in experiment one. All subjects failed to do anything with the occluder. Varied 'out of sight condition' were administered. 'The manikin was presented on the end of a string, dangling in front of the baby. Before the baby could reach out for the toy, the room lights were extinguished ... The toy was thus out of sight ... The babies' behaviour was observed with ... TV system ... The babies were left alone in darkness for three minutes. At the end of this time the standard object permanence test was repeated', p. 170.

RESULTS / No subject passed the standard object permanence test on either presentation. All subjects were able to reach out to obtain the object out of sight in darkness. 'The hands went straight to the object locus ... even after initial periods of distress testing as long as 90 seconds', p. 170.

The relationship between the cognitive and linguistic pluralization rules in 18—38 month-old children
B.S.P. Coffman, 1975

AIM / To discover empirical evidence in support of the hypothesis that language abilities are based on cognitive abilities 'by showing that the child possessed a cognitive equivalent of a linguistic structure prior to either the comprehension or production of the structure.'

SUBJECTS / N = 32 between the ages of 18 and 38 months.

METHOD / Two tasks were administered: a cognitive and a linguistic task. The former comprised of hiding a raisin in one of two small boxes. S could distinguish the appropriate box by noting whether the figure on its lid appeared in the singular or plural. 'The singular was defined as one occurence of the figure, the plural as two occurrences. Three variations on the "one versus two" distinction were used with the intent of exploring the progressive cognitive levels in the child's acquisition of the plural schema.' The linguistic task comprised of presenting pairs of 3xs cards 'with one and two occurrences of the same figure and asking the child to either choose or describe one of the pair. Variations on the linguistic task consisted of the use of the marked number modifier "two" and the use of real versus nonsense vocabulary items.'

RESULTS / The three youngest age groups had significantly higher scores on the cognitive than the linguistic task. The author interpreted the results as 'offering strong support for the Piagetian hypothesis that language is built on broader intellectual schemas and is not an innately programmed function. The oldest age group, however, presented some unexpected results. Its participants were not significantly more successful on the cognitive than the linguistic task. These results, although nonsignificant, were viewed as being indicative of a change in the child's preferred mode of intellectual operations. Further expansion of Piagetian theory to include such mode preference was proposed.'

Enhancement of hidden object search in six-month-old infants presented with a continuously sounding hidden object
H.J. Ginsburg and D.L. Wong, 1973

Infants who fail to search for a hidden object during the third stage of the sensorimotor in spite of an auditory signal of its presence have been noted by Piaget (1954).

AIM / The authors sought to determine if the continued presence of a sounding stimulus would foster an infant's search for that stimulus when concealed from view.

SUBJECTS / N = 8. Five male and three female infants of middle class background were involved in the study.

METHOD / All Ss demonstrated a lack of ability to search for nonsounding hidden objects. 'In Phase one ... each subject was presented with a non-sounding Plexiglas music box (9 x 9 x 14 centimeters). After the subject had handled the music box it was removed from his grasp, placed directly in front of the seated infant, and slowly covered with a white cotton cloth. The covering always occurred from the back of the object to the front in relation to the infant. Phase two was identical to the first phase except that the music box sounded continuously from the time just before presentation to the infant until after the object was completely concealed. Phase three was identical to phase one; all phases consisted of three trials.' Details of the scoring techniques are described elsewhere (Ginsburg and Wong, 1973, p. 142).

RESULTS / Differences in response between sounding and nonsounding trials were statistically significant (sign test, p = .016, one − tailed). 'Results are considered in the context of the possible orienting effect produced by the continuous auditory signal of the object's presence which served to maintain the infant's attention throughout the entire concealment procedure', p. 142.

Piaget's stage IV object concept error − evidence of forgetting or object conception?
G. Gratch, K.J. Appel, W.F. Evans, G.K. LeCompte and N.A. Wright, 1974

AIM / The authors maintain that Piaget (1954) has argued that the AB error occurs because infants fail to assimilate the information that the object is hidden in a new place. Their study evaluates the relative merits of the forgetting and the failure to register explanations of the AB phenomenon.
(Infants aged nine months are able to find an object hidden under a cover when it is hidden in one place, A, but they err by searching once again at A when they see the object hidden at a second place, B. This phenomenon, is termed, AB error).

SUBJECTS / N = 48, with an age range from seven months 13 days to ten months and 16 days. Twenty were from lower class, mainly Negro and 28 were middle class and primarily white.

METHOD / Twelve subjects were assigned to each of the one of four delay groups, o, one, three, or seven sec. The apparatus consisted of a tray with two wells spaced 12 inches apart. Two 12 x 12 inch white washcloths served as covers and a gold-coloured bell was used as the toy.

A trials — 'with the tray positioned so that it was out of reach of subject experimenter brought the toy close to subject. As subject began to reach for it, experimenter slowly moved the toy to the A well, directing subjects reach toward that side. While subject was attending to the toy in the well, experimenter slowly covered the well with the cloth . . . when the toy was covered, experimenter depressed a foot pedal which activated a small light located behind subject, and experimenter responded to the onset of the light by slowly sliding the tray within subjects reach. If subject found the toy, he was allowed to play with it for about 10 sec. before the next trial. If subject searched at the wrong side, he was allowed to correct his error or was corrected by experimenter. The subject had to succeed on five consecutive A trials before the toy was hidden at B', p. 73.

B trials — The same delay conditions were followed in B trials as in A trials = 7_A sec. 7_B sec. All subjects had five trials at the B side. 'If subject searched at A on any of the B trials, the tray was pulled back before subject had an opportunity to search at B. The experimenter then drew subjects attention to the B well, uncovered it, and handed the toy to subject. If subject had not found the toy at B on the fourth and fifth trials, the B trials were continued until subject found the toy twice in succession', p 73.

Ratings included whether the infant attended to the hiding wells (attentiveness); the particular well he directed his attention (direction of gaze); the period of time after the toy was covered and before the tray was moved within subjects reach (delay); the period that began when experimenter moved the hiding tray and terminated by subjects uncovering of a hiding well (presentation).

RESULTS / The authors conclude, 'Piaget explains the Stage IV error as a failure to assimilate the new place of hiding rather than a forgetting of it. His hypothesis predicts that the likelihood of error should not vary with the length of the delay interval . . . infants were delayed o, one, three or seven sec. before having the opportunity to search. Infants in all conditions, save 10 sec. were likely to err. While Piaget's hypothesis was not supported by the results of the o-sec. condition, subsequent analysis of the data provided some support for Piaget's hypothesis', p. 71. The results are discussed with Piaget's (1954) findings and Harris (1973). The latter proposed that the error may be explained in terms of pro-active inhibition. While the authors lend support to Harris's interpretation, they 'would like to suggest that a modified version of Piaget's hypothesis may provide a better account of these errors', p. 77.

The development of object permanence in the cat
H.E. Gruber, J.S. Girgus, and A. Banuazizi, 1971

AIM / To examine the development of behaviours related to object permanence in the cat.

SUBJECTS / N = 26. The sample comprised four kittens aged 10 to 12 weeks in Group One; four cats aged 24 to 26 weeks in Group Two; four cats aged 108 to 110 weeks in Group Three. These were all laboratory-raised kittens and cats. The fourth group consisted of seven house-reared kittens aged 10 to 12 weeks. Additionally 'data were gathered from three house-reared littermates between the ages of six days and 10 weeks, and from a second litter of four house-reared littermates between the ages of 13 weeks and 30 weeks', p. 10.

METHOD / Eight modified test situations were employed patterned after Piaget (1954) as follows: (i) Auditory stimulus (clock) off to one side; (2) Object swung in circle around kitten; (3) Object placed in front of kitten and moved slightly; (4) Object and kitten placed on stool; (5) Kitten playing with object − auditory distraction introduced; (6) Kitten playing with object − visual distraction introduced; (7) Kitten is distracted from playing with object − object is covered while kitten is distracted (8) Object is covered while kitten is playing with it.
(Details are described in Gruber, Girgus and Banuazizi, 1971, p. 10)

RESULTS / The authors conclude, 'In a study of laboratory-reared animals, it was found that cats reach an early developmental limit; unlike children, they are unable to follow an object through a series of invisible displacements. House-reared cats showed similar limitations, but advanced more rapidly than cage-reared animals . . . longitudinal study suggests that cats go through four stages rather than the six found by Piaget in children. In the first 24 weeks of life, kittens develop as far as children do in their first year, but the child's behaviour with respect to vanished objects eventually becomes more complex and more general', p. 9.

*Perseverative search at a visibly empty place by young infants**
P.L. Harris

Experiment One

AIM / The author was intent to study perseverative search at a visibly empty place in young infants.

SUBJECTS / N = 12 infants with a mean age of 364 days.

METHOD / 'Infants were first given the toy car to manipulate. Once interest was aroused the infant's mother pushed open one of the Plexiglas doors and placed the car behind it. Infants were then encouraged to retrieve it. Following two such successful warm up trials, the car was handed to the E seated behind the screen who placed it in the centre of the Plexiglas window. As soon as the infant was fixating the car, it was pushed forward by the E so that the sloping track carried it to its resting place behind one of the Plexiglas doors. The infant could then retrieve it as before; After three such pre-test trials infants were given two test trials, for which both doors were blocked. For pre-test and test trials, the infant's mother was asked not to encourage or direct the infant in any way. Half the Ss received all pre-test trials at the left-hand door and half received them at the right. All infants were given one test trial with the object at the same door as pre-test trials (A trial) and one test trial with the object at the new door (B trial). The order of the test trials was counterbalanced across Ss. Each trial lasted for 90 sec with an intertrial interval of approximately 10 sec', p. 537.

Experiment Two

AIM / To examine the developmental origin of search at an empty location.

SUBJECTS / N = 28 infants. Fourteen younger infants had a mean age of 307 days and 14 older infants had a mean age of 383 days.

METHOD / The experimental procedure was similar to that used for experiment one apart from minor modifications. A single test trial was administered at door B which was opaque — door A remained transparent. The car was removed by the E, following its disappearance at door B. Both doors could be pushed open. 'Displacement of either door activated a timer-counter. For half the Ss door A was to the right, door B to the left, for the remaining Ss the reverse was the case', p. 539.

---

* Gratitude is extended to Dr P.L. Harris of the University of Lancaster for sending his work to be abstracted.

RESULTS / That even where infants register the objects new location they still remember and approach its prior location. 'These object locations are not mutually exclusive for the infant even when the object is visible at one but not the other. Thus, while it may be accurate to describe the infant as vulnerable to interference from stored information (Harris, 1973), this occurs for new object locations which are visible as well as remembered. Hence the hypotheses of proactive interference in short-term memory must be revised. Interference obtains for perceived and stored locations', pp. 540–541.

Task characteristics and a stage six sensorimotor problem
C.B. Kopp, M.J. O'Connor and I. Finger, 1975

AIM / To determine whether modifying the task characteristics of the problem (Casati and Lezine, 1968), by introducing additional visual clues by use of a transparent tube, helped operativity in infants.

Experiment One
SUBJECTS / N = 80 within the age range from 20 to 33 months.

METHOD / The material comprised a plastic toy rake and two cylindrical plastic tubes. One tube was painted red and was opaque, the other was colourless and transparent. Each S was showed one of the tubes, with the instructions, 'There is a cookie inside the tube. Can you get it?' The S was unable to reach the cookie with his fingers. 'The tube was placed in front of the child with the rake positioned diagonally across the top of the tube. The child was allowed up to three 60-sec. presentations of each stimulus to solve the problem. If the solution was obtained within the first two presentations, testing was ended for that trial. All presentations of the same stimulus constituted a trial. Each child was presented with the opaque and transparent tubes. In order to balance for presentation order effects, half of the children received the opaque tube on trial one followed by the transparent tube on trial two (order one). The other half were presented the tubes in reversed order (order two)', p. 570.

Experiment Two
SUBJECTS / N = 80 ranging in age from 28 to 34 months.

METHOD / The experimental procedure was the same as for experiment one, above.

RESULTS / Problem solving was facilitated in the transformed condition, with older Ss performing at higher levels than younger Ss. The authors suggested that 'cognitive requirements of the problem, as representative of stage six sensorimotor development, remained the same in the original or transformed condition. The modification appeared to permit children to focus their attention on the requirements of the problem, so that a greater number of children demonstrated mental representation. Task characteristics of sensorimotor problems need to be investigated further', Kopp, O'Connor, and Finger (1975, p. 569).

Ordinality and sensorimotor series
C.B. Kopp, M. Sigman, and A.H. Parmelee, 1973

Corman and Escalona (1969) demonstrated near-perfect ordinality for the object-permanence and space series that they used. Likewise, Uzgiris and Hunt (1966) reported near-perfect scalability for their object-permanence series. However, Miller, Cohen and Hill (1970) did not fully substantiate these findings. More recently, Uzgiris and Hunt (1972) also reported ordinality data for the seven series of their sensorimotor test.

AIM / To demonstrate that ordinality of sensorimotor series may be influenced by developmental change.

SUBJECTS / N = 24. Withn the age range nine to 20 months and with middle class background.

METHOD / The sensorimotor series utilized were developed by Casati and Lézine (1968). The search for the hidden object test was similar to those used by Gouin-Décarie, 1965 and Uzgiris and Hunt, (1966). 'The other area of performance evaluated is called "use of intermediaries" and examines the child's ability to "see" a relationship between two objects in pursuit of a goal. One of the objects, a toy desired by the infant, is distant from him and accessible only by manipulation of an intermediary object that is nearby. The intermediaries consist of strings or a cloth and pivot. The two sub-tests in this performance area are called "use of extension of the object" (strings) and "use of the relationship between object and support" (cloth and pivot). Some of the items in these two tests are similar to items in the series called "Development of Means for Obtaining Events" developed by Uzgiris and Hunt', p. 822.

RESULTS / Green's (1956) index of consistency was utilized to evaluate ordinality of the three sub-tests of the sensorimotor series. Ordinality was affected by the age and concomitant abilities of the subjects. Moreover, scalability differed in the different sub-tests administered.

Longitudinal study of sensorimotor development
C. B. Kopp, M. Sigman, and A. H. Parmelee, 1974

AIMS / The authors formulated three questions as follows: (a) What was the rate of acquisition of different kinds of sensorimotor behaviours? (b) How much variability was noted in performance? (c) What relationships did the various subtests have with each other for the single category of infant studied?

SUBJECTS / N = 24 full-term Caucasian infants, with the developmental quotients ranging from 98, to 126 (Gesell Developmental Schedules), with a mean of 110.5 and a standard deviation of 8.6. Attrition of numbers was caused by three families leaving the project after five or more testing sessions. The data from these infants however, were kept in the study.

METHOD / Using the 'Stages of Sensorimotor Intelligence in the Child', (Casati and Lézine, 1968), sensorimotor behaviours were assessed. The series consists of four areas: (a) Search for the hidden object is a subtest that studies the S's awareness of the existence of an object when it is covered and subsequent displacements of the object in time and space. The subtest is based, in part, on Gouin-Décarie's (1967) work; (b) Use of intermediaries in a subtest that assesses the infant's ability to 'see' a relationship between two objects; (c) Exploration of objects is a single subtest that examines the child's ability to separate followed by integrating components of an object; (d) Combination of objects is a test that evaluates the infant's ability to invent a solution to solve a problem. Experimental procedures were similar to Casati and Lézine (1968) and fuller details are also described elsewhere, Kopp, Sigman and Parmelee (1974, pp. 688–689).

RESULTS / The study demonstrated that infants studied on the four sensorimotor behaviours on the Casati and Lézine (1968) test showed overall progression in stage development; occasional regressions in performance occurred and were related to the infant's age; and performance on one subtest was generally unrelated to performance on another subtest. 'Performance decline or instability of responses appears to be a characteristic of infant development (Bayley, 1949). King and Seegmiller (1973), in recent longitudinal study of black male infants 14 to 22 months old, also reported some score decrement at all tested ages on the Bayley infant test, but the largest decrease occurred between the 14- and 18-month testings. There are a number of factors that could account for the discrepancy between the King and Seegmiller (1973) data and the present research, which found instability of responses to be most prevalent between 12 and 15 months. These factors include use of different tests, examiners, and subjects. However, in view of the findings of both studies, one could conclude that assignment of a test score to infants between 12 and 18 months may not be an adequate reflection of the infant's abilities', Kopp, Sigman, and Parmelee (1974, p. 694).

Infants' development of object permanence: a refined methodology and new evidence for Piaget's hypothesized ordinality
J.A. Kramer, K.T. Hill, and L.B. Cohen, 1975

AIM / To investigate Piaget's theory of object concept development.

SUBJECTS / N = 30 infants ranging in age from five to 32 months. Half the Ss were drawn from a day-care centre while the remaining half were cared for at home throughout the year.

METHOD / Six of the 16 object permanence tasks developed by Uzgiris and Hunt (1974) and used by Miller *et al.* (1970) were selected. It was expected that task one would be least difficult and task six most difficult. Task one (task three in Miller *et al.*) was to find an object partially hidden under one of three screens. Task two (task seven in Miller *et al.*) was to find an object hidden under one of three screens. Task three (task eight in Miller *et al.*) was to find an object after successive visible displacements. Task four (task nine in Miller *et al.*) was to find an object hidden under three superimposed screens. Task five (task 14 in Miller *et al.*) was to find an object after one invisible displacement. Task six (task 15 in Miller *et al.*) was to find an object after successive invisible displacements. In summary, five variables were of interest: sex of child, age, environment, sessions, and tasks.

RESULTS / Clear evidence was computed for task ordinality as proposed by Piaget, with ordinality coefficients ranging from .71 to .82 for the three testing sessions. Performance changes across the three sessions were likewise ordinal in 80 per cent of the cases. Expected age, task, and session effects and accompanying interactions were also noted.

Twins: concordance for Piagetian-equivalent items derived from the Bayley Mental Test
A.P. Matheny, 1975

AIM / By analyzing performance on Piagetian-equivalent tasks from infant tests given to twins during their first year, an attempt was made to find which aspects of sensorimotor capabilities might reveal concordance for genetically related pairs.

SUBJECTS / 120 identical pairs of twins and 85 same-sex fraternal pairs of twins at ages three, six, nine, and 12 months. Twins were identified by bloodtyping (Wilson, 1970) as being identical or fraternal pairs.

METHOD / Three judges independently studied the description of Piagetian items on scales devised by Escalona and Corman (1967) and by Uzgiris and Hunt (1968). A list of Bayley items from the mental test as described in the manual for the Bayley Scales of Infant Development (Bayley, 1969), which seemed most analogous to items found on the Piagetian scales was compiled. 'For the most part, the mental test items that were selected were comparable to items found on the scales by Uzgiris and Hunt; however items classified under prehension were analogous to those found on the scales by Escalona and Corman,. . . The completed list consisted of 20 Bayley mental test items representing behaviours pertaining to the following scales: (a) prehension, (b) object permanence, (c) means-ends, (d) space, and (e) imitation', p. 225. 8

RESULTS / Identical twin pairs were found to be consistently more concordant than fraternal twin pairs, the highest levels of significance being computed at three and six months, and for items related to prehension, object permanence, and imitation. Within pair correlations for the total score were .80 for identical pairs and .61 for fraternal pairs; these correlations were significantly different. The findings substantiated Piaget's assertions regarding the biological origins of sensorimotor capabilities. The author concluded with a discussion of the expectations for differential utility for infant scales constructed from Piagetian concepts as opposed to other infant measures.

A longitudinal study of representational play in relation to spontaneous imitation and development of multi-word utterances. *
L. McCune Nicolich and J.B. Raph, 1975

The purpose of this investigation was to examine the level of symbolic capability as revealed in play, the use of spontaneous vocal imitation and its relationship to symbolic level, and the nature of certain classes of words occurring in spontaneous language. These three facets of child behaviour were examined during the period of single-word utterances and early multi-word combinations with a view of elucidating certain cognitive aspects of early language.

Evidence regarding the sequential development of symbolic play has been suggested in the theoretical literature by Piaget (1962) and Bruner, Olver, and Greenfield (1966). This phenomenon has also been demonstrated by Sinclair (1970). The functions of spontaneous vocal imitation have been explored by Bloom, Hood, and Lightbown (1973) to determine how imitation leads to lexical development and the development of semantic-syntactic relations in language. Lezine (1971, unpublished) suggested that coordinations in play behaviour constitute the roots of logico-mathematical structures. Bloom (1973) demonstrated that certain single-word utterances code relationships in the environment.

Specifically, this study examined the following variables: level of symbolic play, use of spontaneous vocal imitation, and cognitive aspects of certain word classes. The temporal sequencing of development in these areas was then compared. Concomitantly, methodological refinements were called for to establish symbolic play levels as a system for yielding reliable levels of cognitive development emerging late in the sensorimotor period. Further, there was a need for research beginning earlier in language acquisition, and thus extending for a longer period of development than had previously been reported for these particular variables. Children in this study were observed from the early part of the single-word period, until multi-word utterances comprised 25 per cent of their language in a given sample. At the time of initial observation, they had achieved the sixth sensorimotor stage (Corman and Escalona, 1969).

Five female subjects ranging in age from 14 to 19 months at the time the study began were observed monthly in the home for 40-minute periods over a one-year time span. The children were presented with a standard set of toys and engaged in free play and conversation with

* Written and prepared by the authors for inclusion in this volume.
Gratitude is extended to Drs Lorraine McCune Nicholich and Jane Beasley Raph of Rutgers University, the State University of New Jersey.

their mothers. These sessions were videotaped, transcribed, and the following analyses performed.

The videotape was divided into play episodes, each of which was judged and assigned a symbolic play level as suggested by Piaget (1962). Reliability of coding was .85, significant at .05 level. The language and contextual information were transcribed and child utterances compared to preceding maternal utterances to determine whether the utterances were imitative. The non-naming words used by each child for three or more sessions were identified. The contextual material included in the transcripts was then examined to determine whether conditions accompanying the occurrence of the identified words justified their inclusion in the action-judgment class.

The following results were obtained:

1. Children progressed through the play levels at varying paces, but in the order described by Piaget.

2. All children used vocal imitation, following a similar functional form $y = Ax^{Bе^{Cx}}$ where y is imitation rate and x is age. The fit to this regression equation was significant for four children at level .05, the fifth at .06. The proportion of imitation varied extensively over time for each subject. Words were selectively imitated during the course of the study moving from imitated to spontaneous use.

3. The extent of vocal imitation was a function of symbolic development. The maximum of the predicted vocal imitation function occurred at a relatively consistent symbolic level for all children, as did the later accomplishment of predominantly multi-word language.

4. A small class of single-word utterances was identified which apparently code reversible relations derived from sensorimotor experience and prefiguring operational intelligence. These words as a group were rarely imitated during the course of the investigation.

The major conclusions of this study are that there are consistent patterns of vocal imitative behaviour and of symbolic development. The use of language to code precursors of operational intelligence was remarkably consistent for all children observed. It is suggested that common cognitive skills developed during the sensorimotor period form the foundation for these patterns of development.

Conservation of weight in infants
P. Mounoud and T.G.R. Bower, 1975

AIM / From two series of experiments to make systematic observations of casual observation that conservation of weight, realized through actions is achieved during infancy.

SUBJECTS / N = 60 Experiment One included six groups of five infants aged between six and 16 months. Experiment Two included 30 infants (six each at nine months, 12 months, 15 months, 18 months and 21 months). A further 24 infants (12 each at 15 months and at 18 months) were involved in the conservation experiment alone.

METHOD / In Experiment One the arm tension experiment was intended to determine whether the baby was capable of adapted differentiated responses to weight, whether or not these responses were cued by visual size and a conservation test. In Experiment Two, the force of grip experiment, anticipations were similar: that expectation that 'the same object would weigh the same on repeated presentations would show up as increasingly precise initial applied pressure over the three presentations of an object, that serial anticipation would show up as increasingly precise initial applied pressure with objects presented late in the series, that lack of conservation would show up as a change in the pressure applied to a transformed object which could increase or decrease depending on whether the baby centers on the variation in length or width. Conservation would appear as no effect of transformation in either direction? (Full details of experimental approaches are given in Mounoud and Bower, 1975, pp. 31 − 32 and p. 38)

RESULTS / The experiments indicated that 'infants develop a behavioural form of weight conservation, the ability to detect that weight is invariant under transformations of the shape of the object whose weight is in question, by 18 months.' The authors comment that the sequence of development is the same as that observed at a verbal level in children between 4 and 8 years. Further, that 'it would seem that we are dealing with the first phase of a vertical *décalage*', (Piaget, 1941b). (Full discussion of the results appear in Mounoud and Bower, 1975, pp. 32−37 and pp. 38−40)

*Play and language: the development of representational thought in infancy**
D. Rosenblatt, 1975

Although several studies have probed the development of manipulative skills in infancy (McCall, 1974; Collard, 1971) and the

* Written and prepared by the author for inclusion in this volume.
Gratitude is extended to Dr Deborah Rosenblatt of Bedford College of the University of London.

beginnings of language (Nelson, 1973; Greenfield, 1973), there is as yet no empirical research on the early relationship between cognition and language, and in particular, the emergence of conceptual abilities which mark the transition from 'sensorimotor' and 'representational' thought. Piaget (1952) suggests that conceptual schemas are directly related to the sign systems, but this has not been confirmed in a normative sample. For this reason 20 infants (5 m.c. boys/girls; 5 w.c. boys/girls) were visited at home monthly between 9 and 18 months, and once again at 24 months in an investigation of toys play strategies, language acquisition, and other representational skills (imitation, categorization, seriation, and object permanence). Twenty simple sensorimotor (based on Piaget's (1952) categories), and 100 symbolic, play behaviours were time-sampled (5 sec.) for 10 minutes with a pre-selected set of toys, and the sessions were tape recorded to recover measures of infant speech. A mother-infant play session of 10 minutes was observed in the same way at 9, 12, 15, 18, 24m. from which maternal speech and play behaviours were derived. Mothers kept extensive diary records of imitation and the first 50 words of their child, with particular attention to the progression of meaning for each word.

Analysis of the play data shows a steady progression from simple play (banging, waving, etc.) with a single toy at 9m. (95 per cent) and no symbolic play, to the predominance of symbolic play (60 per cent) at 18m., as well as simple and symbolic combinations. By 24m. almost all play is symbolic (85 per cent), a high proportion of this (40 per cent) being toys combined into symbolic sequences (pouring tea into cups and then serving it). Whereas 52 per cent of the responses at 9m. are immature and inappropriate (mouthing every toy), this decreases to 5 per cent by 18m. while investigative behaviour (visual inspection, turning, etc.) decreases from 40 per cent to 20 per cent, and appropriate toy use (pushing the car) increases from 2 per cent to 75 per cent. Preference for brightly coloured complex toys between 9 and 13m. yields to selection of duller less complex toys if they have a social or symbolic function by 17m. Between 9 and 18m. specific responses tend to peak and then diminish (mouthing at 9 and 10m., waving between 10 and 13 m., nesting and stacking between 13 and 16). Significant sex differences emerge in toy selection, behavioural responses, and rate of acquisition of symbolic strategies, but social class differences are minimal.

Measures of play behaviour are significantly correlated with language development, such that children who have early symbolic play also show faster word acquisition and a wider range of referents and word types. Early talkers also achieve object permanence earlier and use more advanced sorting strategies, but not better seriation ability. Most measures of maternal speech are not correlated with the children's play behaviour and sorting abilities, but are related to measure of child language. Girls are faster in most aspects of language development, although maternal speech to girls is similar to that of boys; social class differences are not evident in child or maternal speech.

These results suggest that early language (i.e. one-word utterances) is part of the development of a general referential system which bridges sensorimotor and representational thought. The ability to select and order responses, and to apply differentiated and appropriate responses to objects precedes, and then parallels the selection of categories and meanings in the first set of words. Maternal language and play style are two strategic pressures on the child's initial vocabulary, which are complemented by the child's early play behaviour thus determining his semantic development.

Piaget's constructionist theory
D. Smillie, 1972

The author critically examined Piaget's theory of the construction of the object in infancy. Smillie begins by providing a detailed account of Piaget's theory of the development of the infant's conception of the permanent object followed by his critique. He cites the work of Gouin-Décarie (1965), Gratch and Landers (1971) and Piaget's own evidence. Bowers (1966) experiments and results are described in length followed by an overall discussion and an alternative interpretation. (The above studies have received full treatment in Modgil, 1974, Chapter Two).

Smillie asserts, 'It is found that (Piaget's) notion of "perceptual tableaux", used to describe the experience of the young infant, is contradicted by the evidence of Bower's experiments. Reinterpreting Piaget's evidence, support is found for an initial period of visual realism followed by a period in which the infant explores the possibilities of his own actions. Following these substages the infant coordinates the information obtained from vision and manipulation. This interpretation involves a shift of emphasis rather than a total rejection of Piaget's theory. . . .' p. 171. 'The behaviour of the fourth stage illustrates the beginning exploration of the efficacy of intentional action rather than the residue of the infant's initial egocentricity. When the infant has several successes in finding an object in a particular location, there may be a shift in attention away from the perceptual cues toward the effects of the action as such. The reinforcements of an activity (success at position A) leads to the repetition of the act. This pattern should be understood as an aspect of progressive exploration on the part of the infant in which he is trying out behaviour to see what will happen, rather than as a lingering effect of the perceptual tableaux', p. 185.

Patterns of cognitive development in infancy
I.C. Uzgiris, 1973

AIM / The author examines the relationship between levels of object concept construction and achievements in several other branches of functioning.

SUBJECTS / N = 12. The infants were observed in their own homes at weekly intervals starting at four weeks of age up to eight months, at bi-weekly intervals from eight months to 12 months, and at monthly intervals up to 24 or 25 months of age. All subjects were normal, healthy infants at age and from middle class homes.

METHOD / The Scale of Visual Pursuit and the Permanence of Objects (Uzgiris and Hunt, 1966) was administered. This consists of a sequence of 14 steps 'marking progress in the development of the object concept rather than the six levels described as stages by Piaget. However, the critical achievements for each of Piaget's stages appear as steps in our scale, and . . . permit a translation of the infant's level of development into one of Piaget's stages. The infants achievements in other branches of psychological development were also studied using the other scale . . . (a) the Development of Means for Obtaining Desired Environmental Events Scale, which is directed toward assessing the ways in which infants select actions from their repertoire, incorporate perceived relationships between objects in their actions, and use other available objects as means in order to achieve a desired goal; (b) the Construction of Object Relations in Space Scale . . . designed to assess the infant's understanding of the spatial arrangements between objects located in his immediate surround or moving through familiar space; and (c) the Operational Causality Scale . . . designed to assess the way in which infants attempt to cause a reoccurrence of various events and . . . reveal their conception of the cause of those events', p. 185.

RESULTS / Four levels in object concept development were observed. 'The first appears to parallel Piaget's stage three and seems to reflect a minimal level of ability to incorporate perceptually absent objects or events into ongoing schemes of action. The second level appears to span stages four and five in Piaget's system and seems to reflect an increasing differentiation of objects substantiation of objects and contribute to the use of objects as means for achieving desired goal. The third level appears to coincide with the beginning of Piaget's stage six, evidenced by search for an object hidden by means of an invisible displacement, and seems to be achieved subsequent to considerable exploration of the relationships between objects in space. This level probably reflects the articulation of a matrix of spatial relations in which displacements of objects may be envisioned and which makes possible the exploitation of perceived relations between objects for achieving desired goal. The final level coincides with the culmination of the sensorimotor period and reflects the achievement of the ability to represent the displacement of independently moving objects within a spatial framework,' p. 200.

Uzgiris finally concludes by suggesting future possibilities for research and cites the work of Charlesworth (1966). Gratch and Landers (1971), Schofield and Uzgiris (1969) and Bell (1970).

Development of object permanence in the infant squirrel monkey
R.M. Vaughter, W. Smotherman, and J.M. Ordy, 1972

AIM / The authors were intent to investigate the development of the object concept in infant squirrel monkeys as it related to response training.

SUBJECTS / N = 4. Three infant male squirrel monkeys were respectively six, nine and 12 months. A mature squirrel monkey also participated in some problems.

METHOD / The apparatus used was a modification of the Wisconsin General Test (Olsen, Cross and Vaughter, 1966). The experimental procedures were patterned after Rumbaugh (1968) and Rumbaugh and McCormick (1967).

Response training: Pre-test. 'A three-trial problem shaping procedure, typically employed with monkeys in the Wisconsin General Test Apparatus was followed (Rumbaugh and McCormick, 1967; Schrier, Harlow, and Stollnitz, 1965). The purpose of the procedure was to train the S to displace a plain adaptation block which covered one of the foodwells to obtain a reward, a piece of banana'.

Object-Permanence Task. Twenty test trials a day for 5 days were administered. 'A test trial occurred every third trial according to the three-step response-training . . . except that on all trials, the foodwell was baited in plain view of the S'. The mature female monkey was tested on this task.

Object-Overpermanence Task. E's actions took place in full view of the subject as in the object-permanence task. 'Identical adaptation blocks covered each of two peripheral foodwells at the outset of each trial . . . and E (a) placed food in one well and covered it with one of the blocks and (b) then transferred the food from that well, the block being replaced over the first well, to the second foodwell, which was then covered by the second block . . . S was allowed 30 seconds to respond . . . An overpermanence response was defined as the S's displacement of the block under which the food had been placed originally'. The mature female monkey was tested on this task.

Response Training: Post-test. This was identical to the pre-test. (Fuller details of all the tasks including the experimental procedures and the apparatus are described elsewhere — Vaughter, Smotherman, and Ordy, 1972, pp. 34—36.)

RESULTS / The authors conclude, 'The typical Wisconsin General Test Apparatus response-training procedures assume that the subject, from the outset, has a fully developed object concept: the object concept develops in the infant squirrel monkey: and the development of object permanence in the infant squirrel monkey generally follows along the sequence described by Piaget', p. 34.

Information and strategy in the young child's search for hidden objects
R.A. Webb, B. Massar, and T. Nadolny, 1972

AIM / The study attempted to test the information and strategy in the child's search for hidden objects.

SUBJECTS / N = 40. Twenty of the subjects ranged in age from 13 months three weeks to 14 months one week and 20 ranged in age from 15 months three weeks to 16 months one week.

METHOD / 'Three sets of delayed-reaction problems were seen in which the child was asked to locate an object hidden in one of three places after a delay of five, 10 or 15 seconds . . . On the first set . . . a plastic Pooh Bear or a ping-pong ball was hidden under one of three green cups three inches in diameter and three-and-a-half inches tall. A delay of five seconds was used. In the second set . . . ,using a delay of ten seconds, a bracelet was hidden in one of three drawers in a $3\frac{1}{4}$ x $3\frac{1}{4}$ x 4 inch toy chest. Finally . . . , a plastic Fred Flintstone was hidden under one of three quart-size plastic containers five inches in diameter and $4\frac{7}{8}$ inches tall, and the child was delayed for 15 seconds before starting his search', p. 93. All trials were administered in the same manner. (Fuller details of the experimental procedure are described in Webb, Massar, and Nadolny, 1972, pp. 93—94).

RESULTS / The authors conclude '16- and 14-month old children were studied in three-choice delayed-reaction problems. Sixteen-month-olds were able to locate a hidden object correctly on initial trials but made subsequent errors due to a tendency to return to a previous location. The majority of these children, however, located the object correctly with their second choice. Fourteen-month-olds were less successful . . . data indicate that the information from the hiding remained effective even while the child was making his initial error', p. 91. The authors interpret the findings in terms of search strategy and memory.

Piagetian object permanence in the infant rhesus monkey
K.L. Wise, L.A. Wise and R.R. Zimmermann, 1974

AIM / An investigation of object permanence was undertaken in a longitudinal study of infant monkeys in a human analogue testing situation and two sub-human analogue testing situations.

Study One
SUBJECTS / N = 2 male rhesus monkeys (Subjects 37 and 38). The subjects were housed in individual metal cages and different set of four toys was placed in each subjects cage biweekly. The subjects were five days of age when removed from their mother and solid foods given when aged 30 days.

METHOD / 'All of the trials involved presenting the subject with an object or objects, one of which was the test object, and performing some manipulation with the objects. The subjects behaviour was observed for a specified time, and each trial was evaluated as either a plus trial or a minus trial. In a plus (correct response), all the apparatus was removed except the test object, and the subject was allowed an additional 30 seconds to interact with the test object . . . if the subject received a minus, all the apparatus, including the test object was removed', p. 430.

Object permanence was studied through tasks and procedures designed to be analogues of those tasks employed by Piaget (1954) with the child but adapted to the structural and behavioural characteristics of the subjects. The human analogue tasks comprised: (a) Recognition; (b) Assimilation of vision to prehension; (c) Assimilation of prehension to vision; (d) Accommodation to rapid movement; (e) Reconstruction of an invisible whole from a visible fraction (particle displacement); (f) Visible displacement with reaching; (g) Visible displacement; (h) Sequential visible displacement; (i) Successive visible displacement; (j)

Invisible displacement; (k) Sequential invisible displacement; (l) Successive invisible displacement; (m) Superimposed screens. (Details of the experimental procedure are described in Wise, Wise and Zimmermann, 1974, pp. 430—431).

Study Two

SUBJECTS / N = 2 male rhesus monkeys as in study one, above.

METHOD / A Grice-type two-choice discrimination maze apparatus was designed for use in the discrimination maze tasks. These consisted of: (a) Visible displacement; (b) Sequential visible displacement; (c) Successive visible displacement (d) Invisible displacement; (e) Sequential invisible displacement; and (f) Successive invisible displacement. (Details are given in Wise, Wise and Zimmerman, *op. cit.*, pp. 433—434).

The Wisconsin General Test Apparatus Tasks were also administered using a modified Wisconsin General Test Apparatus. The tasks comprised: (a) Visible displacement; (b) Sequential visible displacement; (c) Successive visible displacement; (d) Invisible displacement; (e) Sequential invisible displacement; (f) Successive invisible displacement. (Details are given in Wise, Wise and Zimmermann, *op. cit.*, pp. 434—435).

RESULTS / The study indicated that 'the ages at which certain object-related behaviours were demonstrated by the subjects as stable responses were found by the presentation of tasks that involved various manipulations of objects. In each testing situation was found a sequence of development of object permanence that was very similar to the one described by Piaget for the child, and in each case the sequence culminated in behaviours nearly as complex as those described by Piaget for the two-year old human infant', p. 429.

ABBREVIATIONS USED IN THE BIBLIOGRAPHY
(under the series *Piagetian Research*, Vols. 1–8)

Acta Psychol.	Acta Psychologica (Holland)
Adol.	Adolescence
Aging and Hum. Develop.	Aging and Human Development
Alberta J. Ed. Res.	Alberta Journal of Educational Research
Am. Ed. Res. Assoc.	American Educational Research Association
Am. Ed. Res. J.	American Educational Research Journal
Am. J. Ment. Def.	American Journal of Mental Deficiency
Am. J. Orthopsych.	American Journal of Orthopsychiatry
Am. J. Psych.	American Journal of Psychology
Am. J. Soc.	American Journal of Sociology
Am. Psych.	American Psychologist
Am. Psych. Assoc.	American Psychological Association
Am. Soc. Rev.	American Sociological Review
Ann. Rev. Psych.	Annual Review of Psychology
Arch. Dis. Child.	Archives of the Diseases of Childhood (UK)
Archiv. Gen. Psychiat.	Archives of General Psychiatry
Arch. de Psychol.	Archives de Psychologie
Aust. J. Psych.	Australian Journal of Psychology
Aust. J. Soc. Issues	Australian Journal of Social Issues
Brit. J. Clin. & Soc. Psych.	British Journal of Clinical and Social Psychology
Brit. J. Ed. Psych.	British Journal of Educational Psychology
Brit. J. Psych.	British Journal of Psychology
Brit. J. Stat. Psych.	British Journal of Statistical Psychology
Brit. J. Psych. Stat.	British Journal of Psychology – Statistical Section
Brit. J. Soc.	British Journal of Sociology
Brit. Med. Bull.	British Medical Bulletin
Brit. J. Med. Psych.	British Journal of Medical Psychology
Bull. Danish Inst. for Ed. Res.	Bulletin of the Danish Institute for Educational Research
Calif. J. Ed. Res.	Californian Journal of Educational Research
Can. Educ. Res. Dig.	Canadian Educational and Research Digest
Can. J. Behav. Sci.	Canadian Journal of Behavioural Science
Can. J. Psych.	Canadian Journal of Psychology
Can. Psychol.	Canadian Psychology
Child. Developm.	Child Development (USA)
Child Study Journ.	Child Study Journal
Childhood Psych.	Childhood Psychology (UK)
Cogn.	Cognition
Cogn. Psych.	Cognitive Psychology
Contemp. Psych.	Contemporary Psychology (USA)
Dev. Psych.	Developmental Psychology (USA)

Diss. Abstr.	Dissertation Abstracts (USA)
Educ. of Vis. Handicap.	Education of the Visually Handicapped
Educ. & Psych. Measmt.	Educational and Psychological Measurement (USA)
Ed. Res.	Educational Research (UK)
Ed. Rev.	Educational Review (UK)
Educ. Stud. Maths.	Educational Studies in Mathematics
El. Sch. J.	Elementary School Journal (USA)
Eug. Rev.	Eugenics Review (UK)
Excep. Child.	Exceptional Children
Forum Educ.	Forum Education
Gen. Psych. Mon.	Genetic Psychological Monographs (USA)
Harv. Ed. Rev.	Harvard Educational Review
Human Developm.	Human Development (Switzerland)
Hum. Hered.	Human Heredity
Inst. Child Welf. Monogr.	Institute of Child Welfare Monographs
Int. J. Psych.	International Journal of Psychology (France)
Int. Rev. Educ.	International Review of Education (Germany)
Int. Soc. Sci. Bull.	International Social Science Bulletin (France)
Jap. J. Ed. Psych.	Japanese Journal of Educational Psychology
Jap. Psych. Res.	Japanese Psychological Research
J. Abnorm. Soc. Psych.	Journal of Abnormal and Social Psychology (USA)
Journ. Amer. Acad. Child Psychiat.	Journal of American Academy of Child Psychiatry
J. Am. Stat. Assoc.	Journal of American Statistical Association
J. App. Psych.	Journal of Applied Psychology (USA)
J. Compar. Psychol.	Journal of Comparative Psychology
J. Comp. and Physiolog. Psych.	Journal of Comparative and Physiological Psychology
J. Child Psych. Psychiatr.	Journal of Child Psychology and Psychiatry
J. Clin. Psych.	Journal of Clinical Psychology (USA)
J. Consult. Psych.	Journal of Consultant Psychology (USA)
J. Cross. Cult. Psych.	Journal of Cross-Cultural Psychology (USA)
J. Ed. Psych.	Journal of Educational Psychology (USA)
J. Ed. Res.	Journal of Educational Research (USA)
J. Ed. Stud.	Journal of Educational Studies (USA)
J. Exp. Child Psych.	Journal of Experimental Child Psychology (USA)
J. Exp. Educ.	Journal of Experimental Education
J. Exp. Psych.	Journal of Experimental Psychology

J. Gen. Psych.	Journal of Genetic Psychology (USA)
J. Gerontol	Journal of Gerontology
J. Home Econ.	Journal of Home Economics
Journ. Learn. Disabil.	Journal of Learning Disabilities
J. Math. Psych.	Journal of Mathematical Psychology
J. Ment. Sub.	Journal of Mental Subnormality
J. Negro Ed.	Journal of Negro Education (USA)
J. Pers.	Journal of Personality (USA)
J. Pers. Soc. Psych.	Journal of Personality and Social Psychology (USA)
J. Pers. Assessm.	Journal of Personality Assessment (USA)
J. Psych.	Journal of Psychology (USA)
J. Res. Maths. Educ.	Journal of Research in Mathematics Education
J. Res. Sci. Teach.	Journal of Research in Science Teaching (USA)
J. Soc. Iss.	Journal of Social Issues (USA)
J. Soc. Psych.	Journal of Social Psychology (USA)
J. Soc. Res.	Journal of Social Research
J. Spec. Ed.	Journal of Special Education (USA)
Journ. Struct. Learn.	Journal of Structural Learning
J. Teach. Ed.	Journal of Teacher Education (USA)
J. Verb. Learn. Verb. Behv.	Journal of Verbal Learning and Verbal Behaviour (UK/USA)
J. Youth Adolesc.	Journal of Youth and Adolescence
Math. Teach.	Mathematics Teacher (USA)
Maths. Teach.	Mathematics Teaching
Merr.-Palm. Quart.	Merrill-Palmer Quarterly (USA)
Mon. Soc. Res. Child Dev.	Monographs of the Society for Research in Child Development (USA)
Mult. Beh. Res.	Multivariate Behavioural Research
New Zealand Journ. Educ. Stud.	New Zealand Journal of Educational Studies
Ped. Sem.	Pedagogical Seminary
Pedag. Europ.	Pedogogica Europaea
Percep. Mot. Skills	Perceptual and Motor Skills
Psych. Absts.	Psychological Abstracts
Psych. Afric.	Psychologica Africana
Psych. Bull.	Psychological Bulletin (USA)
Psych. Iss.	Psychological Issues
Psych. Mon.	Psychological Monographs (USA)
Psych. Mon. Gen. and Appl.	Psychological Monographs: General and Applied (USA)
Psychol. Rec.	Psychological Record
Psych. Rep.	Psychological Reports (USA)
Psych. Rev.	Psychological Review (USA)
Psychol. Sch.	Psychology in Schools
Psych. Sci.	Psychological Science (USA)
Psychomet.	Psychometrika
Psy.-nom. Sc.	Psychonomic Science
Psy. Today	Psychology Today
Publ. Opin. Quart.	Public Opinion Quarterly (USA)

Quart. J. Exp. Psych.	Quarterly Journal of Experimental Psychology (UK/USA)
Rev. Educ. Res.	Review of Educational Research
R. Belge de Ps. Ped.	Review Belge de Psychologie et de Pédagogie (Belgium)
Rev. Suisse Psych.	Revue Suisse de Pschologie (Switzerland)
Scan. J. Psych.	Scandinavian Journal of Psychology
Sch. Coun. Curr. Bull.	Schools Council Curriculum Bulletin
Sch. Sci. Maths.	School Science and Mathematics
Sci.	Science
Sci. Americ.	Scientific American
Sci. Ed.	Science Education (USA)
Scot. Ed. Stud.	Scottish Educational Studies
Sem. Psychiat.	Seminars in Psychiatry
Soc. Psychi.	Social Psychiatry
Soviet Psych.	Soviet Psychology
Teach. Coll. Contr. Ed.	Teachers' College Contributions to Education (USA)
Theo. into Pract.	Theory into Practice
Times Ed. Supp.	Times Educational Supplement
Train. Sch. Bull.	Training School Bulletin
Vita. Hum.	Vita Humana
WHO Mon.	World Health Organization Monographs
Wiener Arb. z. pad. Psychol.	Wiener Arbeiten zur pädagogischen Psychologie (Austria)
Yearbook Journ. Negro Educ.	Yearbook of the Journal of Negro Education
Zeitschr. f. ang. Psychol.	Zeitschrift für angewandte Psychologie und Charakterkunde (Germany)
Zeitschr. f. pad. Psychol.	Zeitschrift für pädagogische Psychologie und Fugendkunde (Germany)

BIBLIOGRAPHY

AEBLI, H. (1963) 'Uber die geistige Entwicklung des kindes stuttgart', Klett.

AEBLI, H. (1970) 'Piaget, and beyond', *Interchange*, i, 12–24.

APPEL, K.J., and GRATCH, G. (1969) 'The cue value of objects: Piaget's stages IV and V', paper presented at the meeting of the Soc. for Res. in Child Developm., Santa Monica, California.

ARLIN, P.K. (1975) 'Cognitive development in adulthood: a fifth stage? *Dev. Psych.*, 11, 5, 602–606.

ATHEY, I.J., and RUBADEAU, D.O. (1970) *Educational Implications of Piaget's Theory.* USA: Ginn-Blaisdell.

ATWOOD, G. (1969) 'A developmental study of cognitive balancing in hypothetical three-person systems', *Child Developm.*, 40, 73–85.

BABSKA, Z. (1965) 'The formation of the conception of identity of visual characteristics of objects seen successively'. In: MUSSEN, P.H. (Ed.), 'European Research in Cognitive Development', *Mon. Soc. Res. Child Dev.*, 30, (whole No. 100), 112–24.

BART, W.M., and SMITH, M.B. (1974) 'An interpretive framework of cognitive structures', *Human Developm.*, 17, 161–175.

BAYLEY, N. (1969) *Bayley Scales of Infant Development.* New York: Psychological Corporation.

BEGELMAN, D.A., and STEINFELD, G.J. (1972) 'Is there an error of the standard?: a critique of Piaget's perceptual theory'. *Gen. Psych. Mon.*, 86, 81–117.

BEILIN, H. (1971) In 'Piagetian Cognitive Developmental Research and Mathematical Education', Ed. by M.F. Rosskopf, L.P. Steffe, and S. Taback, Washington: National Council of Teachers of Mathematics.

BELL, S.M. (1968) The relationship of infant-mother attachment to the development of the concept of object permanence. Unpublished PhD dissertation. John Hopkins University.

BELL, S.M. (1970) 'The development of the concept of object as related to infant-mother attachment, *Child Developm.*, 41, 291–311.

BERZONSKY, M.D. (1971) 'Interdependence of Inhelder and Piaget's model of logical thinking', *Dev. Psych.*, 4, 469–476.

BEVER, T.G. (1970) 'The cognitive basis for linguistic structures'. In: HAYES J.R. (Ed.) *Cognition and the Development of Language.* New York: John Wiley & Sons.

BIAGGO, A., WEGNER, G.A., and SIMPSON, C. (1973) 'A developmental study of cognitive dissonance as a function of level of intellectual performance on Piagetian tasks', *Genet. Psycholog. Mon.*, 88, 173—200.

BLANCHARD, E.B., and PRICE, K.C. (1971) 'A developmental study of cognitive balance', *Dev. Psych.*, 5, 344—348.

BLOOM, B. *et al.* (1956) *Taxonomy of Educational Objectives.* New York: David McKay Company.

BOWER, T.G.R. (1966) 'The visual world of infants', *Sci. Amer.*, 215, 80—92.

BOWER, T.G.R. (1967) 'The development of object permanence: some studies of existence constancy', *Percept. Psychophys.*, 2, 411—418.

BOWER, T.G.R. (1971) 'The object in the world of the infant', *Scient. Amer.*, 30—38.

BOWER, T.G.R. (1972) 'Mechanisms of cognitive development in infants'. Colloquim, MIT Psychology Department, May.

BOWER, T.G.R. (1974) *Development in Infancy.* San Francisco: W.H. Freeman.

BOWER, T.G.R. (1974) 'Repetition in human development', *Merr.-Palm. Quart.*, 20, 4, 303—18.

BOWER, T.G.R., and PATERSON, J.G. (1972) 'Stages in the development of the object concept', *Cognition*, 1, 1, 47—55.

BOWER, T.G.R., and PATERSON, J.G. (1973) 'The separation of place, movement and object in the world of the infant', *Journ. Exp. Child Psych.*, 15, 161—168.

BOWER, T.G.R., and WISHART, J.G. (1972) 'The effects of motor skills on object permanence', *Cognition*, 1, 2, 165—171.

BOWER, T.G.R., BROUGHTON, J.M., and MOORE, M.K. (1971) 'Development of the object concept as manifested in changes in the tracking behaviour of infants between seven and 20 weeks of age', *J. Exp. Child Psych.*, 12, 182—193.

BOYLE, D.G. (1969) *A Students' Guide to Piaget.* London: Pergamon Press.

BOYLE, D.G. (1975) 'Has psychology anything to offer the teacher?', personal communication.

BRAINE, M.D.S. (1962) 'Piaget on reasoning: a methodological critique and alternative proposals', *Mon. Soc. Res. Child Dev.*, 27, 41—61.

BRAINERD, C. (1973) The stage problem in behavioural development. Unpublished manuscript, University of Alberta.

BREHM, J.W. (1956) 'Post-decision changes in the desirability of alternatives', *J. Abn. Soc. Psych.*, 52, 384—389.

BROWN, I.E. (1973) A study on the development of the object concept: Inside is not behind. Unpub. MA Thesis. Department of Psychology, Edinburgh University.

BROWN, R.W. (1973) *A First Language: The Early Stages.* Cambridge,

Mass: Harvard Univ. Press.

BRUMER, S. (1975) 'Socio- and psycho-historical factors in the development and growth of a social science: the impact of Jean Piaget on American developmental psychology as a case study; *Diss. Absts.*, 35, 11, 5209B—5726B (5611—B).

BRUNER, J.S. (1959) 'Inhelder and Piaget's The Growth of Logical Thinking: I. A Psychologist's viewpoint', *Brit. J. Psych.*, 50, 363—70.

BRUNER, J.S., OLVER, R.R., and GREENFIELD, P.M. (1966) *Studies in cognitive growth*. New York: Wiley.

BRYANT, P. (1974) *Perception and Understanding in Young Children*. London: Methuen.

BUSS, A.R., and ROYCE, J.R. (1975) 'Ontogenetic changes in cognitive structure from a multivariate perspective', *Dev. Psych.*, 11, 1, 87—101.

BUTTERWORTH, G. (1973) Object permanence during infancy. PhD thesis. Oxford University, England (draft copy).

CASATI, I., and LEZINE, I. (1968) *Les étapes de l'intelligence sensori-motrice*. Paris: Les Editions du Centre de Psychologie Appliquée. (Unpublished translation by E. Ristow).

CASE, R. (1974) 'Structures and strictures: some functional limitations on the course of cognitive growth', *Cogn. Psychol.*, 6, 4, 544—574.

CASE, R. (1974a) 'Mental strategies, mental capacity, and instruction: a neo-Piagetian investigation', *J. Exp. Child Psych.*, 18, 382—389. 382—389.

CASE, R. (1975) 'Social class differences in intellectual development: a neo-Piagetian investigation', *Canad. J. Behav. Sci.*, 7, 3, 244—261.

CASSEL, R.N. (1973) 'Critical contributions of Piaget to developmental Psychology', *Psycholog.*, 10, 1, 42—45.

CASSEL, R.N. (1975) 'Examining Piaget's contributions in relation to humanistic psychology', personal communication. Also Paper presented at the fourth annual international interdisciplinary conference on Piagetian theory and the Helping Professions, Children's Hospital, Los Angeles, California, 24th January.

CATTELL, R.B., and COAN, R.W. (1966) *Guidebook. Early School Personality Questionnaire, 'The ESPQ'*. Champaign, Illinois: Institute of Personality and Ability Testing.

CELLERIER, G. (1972) 'Information processing tendencies in recent experiments in cognitive learning — theoretical implications', In: FARNHAM-DIGGORY S. (Ed.), *Information Processing in Children*. New York: Academic Press.

CHAFE, W.L. (1970) *Meaning and the Structure of Language*. Chicago: University of Chicago Press.

CHARLESWORTH, W.R. (1966) 'Development of the object concept:

a methodological study'. Paper read at Amer. Psycho. Assoc., New York.

COFFMAN, B.S.P. (1975) 'The relationship between the cognitive and linguistic pluralization rules in 18—38 month-old children'. *Diss. Abstrs.*, 35, 11, 5209B—5726B (5659—B)

CORMAN, H., and ESCALONA, S. (1969) 'Stages of sensorimotor development: a replication study', *Merr.-Palm. Quart.*, 15, 351—361.

DAEHLER, M.W. and BUKATKO, D. (1974) 'Discrimination learning in 2 year olds', *Child Developm.*, 45, 378—82.

DAELE, L. VAN DEN (1974) 'Infrastructure and transition in developmental analysis', *Human Developm.*, 17, 1—23.

DASEN, P.R. (1972) 'Cross-cultural Piagetian research: a summary', *J. Cross-Cult. Psych.*, 3, 23—29.

DECARIE, T.G. (1965) *Intelligence and Affectivity in Early Childhood*. New York: International Universities Press.

DIRLAM, D.K. (1972) 'Most efficient chunk sizes'. *Cogn. Psych.*, 3, 335—359.

DIRLAM, D.K. (1973) 'Toward an empirical and rational evaluation of the knowledge process'. St. Norbert College: technical report, November.

DIRLAM, D.K. (1974) The structural analysis of creativity II, Empirical results'. Paper read at the Annual Conference of the Wisconsin Association of Sciences, Arts and Letters, Green Bay, April.

DIRLAM, D.K. (1975) 'Developmental and educational applications of structure theory: a mathematical reformulation of Piaget's concept of Structure', personal communication.

DIRLAM, D.K., and OPITZ, D. (1974c) 'The structural analysis of creativity I. The mathematics of structures'. Paper read at the Annual Conference of the Wisconsin Association of Sciences, Arts and Letters, Green Bay, April.

DIRLAM, D.K., MENDEZ, G., MICHAL, D., and PALM, J. (1974b) 'An application of structure theory to the development of semantic representations'. Paper submitted to *Cognitive Psychology*, November.

DUDEK, S.Z., and DYER, G.B. (1972) 'A longitudinal study of Piaget's developmental stages and the concept of regression I', *J. Pers. Assessm.*, 36, 4, 380—9.

DUDEK, S.Z., LESLIE, E.P., GOLDBERG, J.S., and DYER, G.B. (1969) 'Relationship of Piaget measures to standard intelligence and motor scales', *Percep. Mot. Skills*, 28, 351—62.

EDWARDS, D. (1973) 'Sensory-motor intelligence and semantic

relations in early child grammar', *Cognition*, 2/4, 395—434.

ELKIND, D. (1967) 'Piaget's conservation problems', *Child Developm.*, 38, 15—27.

ELKIND, D. (1970) *Children and Adolescents: Interpretive Essays on Jean Piaget.* Oxford: Oxford University Press.

ESCALONA, S.K., and CORMAN, H.M. (1967) 'The validation of Piaget's hypotheses concerning the development of sensorimotor intelligence: Methodological issues'. Paper presented at the meeting of the Society for Research in Child Development. New York.

EVANS, W.F., and GRATCH, G. (1972) 'The stage IV error in Piaget's theory of object concept development: difficulties in object conceptualization or spatial localization?', *Child Developm.*, 43, 682—88.

FESTINGER, L., and CARLSMITH, J.M. (1959) 'Cognitive consequences of forced compliance', *J. Abn. Soc. Psych.*, 58, 203—210.

FLAVELL, J.H. (1963) *The Developmental Psychology of Jean Piaget.* Princeton, N.J.: Van Nostrand.

FLAVELL, J.H. (1970) 'Cognitive changes in adulthood'. In: GOULET and BALTES, *Life-span Developmental Psychology: Theory and Research*, pp. 248—253. New York: Academic Press.

FLAVELL, J.H. (1971) 'Stage-related properties of cognitive development', *Cogn. Psychol.*, 2, 421—453.

FLAVELL, J.H. (1972) 'An analysis of cognitive-developmental sequences', *Gen. Psych. Mon.*, 86, 279—350.

FLAVELL, J.H., and WOHLWILL, J.F. (1969) 'Formal and functional aspects of cognitive development'. In: ELKIND, D. and FLAVELL, J.H. (Eds.), *Studies in Cognitive Development.* New York: Oxford University Press.

FLEISCHMANN, B., GILMORE, S., and GINSBERG, H. (1966) 'The strength of non-conservation', *J. Exp. Child Psych.*, 4, 353—68.

FURBY, L. (1972) 'Cumulative learning and cognitive development', *Human Developm.*, 15, 265—86.

FURTH, H.G. (1970) *Piaget for Teachers.* Englewood Cliffs, N.J.: Prentice Hall.

GAGNE, R.M. (1968) 'Contributions of learning to human development', *Psych. Rev.*, 3, 177—191.

GANDER, M.J. (1975) 'Conceptual hierarchy theory: a theory of cognitive development', *Diss. Absts.*, 35, 9, 5581A—6281A (5924—A).

GARDNER, H. (1972) *The Quest for Mind: Piaget, Levi-Strauss and the Structuralist Movement.* New York: Random House.

GASCON, J. (1969) Modèle cybernétique d'une sériation de poids chez les enfants . Unpublished Master's thesis, University of Montreal.

GASCON, J. (1969a) Modèle cybernétique d'une sériation de poids. Masters thesis, University of Montreal.

GASCON, J. (1969b) 'Modèle cybernétique d'une sériation de poids chez les enfants', Modeles cybernétiques de la pensee, 2'. Montreal University.

GINSBURG, H.J., and WONG, D.L. (1973) 'Enhancement of hidden object search in six-month-old infants presented with a continuously sounding hidden object', *Dev. Psych.*, 9, 1, 142.

GOLDEN, M., and BIRNS, B. (1968) 'Social class and cognitive development in infancy', *Merr.-Palm. Quart.*, 14, 139—149.

GOLDEN, M., and BIRNS, B. (1971) 'Social class, intelligence and cognitive style in infancy', *Child Developm.*, 42, 2114—2116.

GOODNOW, J. (1962) 'A test of milieu differences with some of Piaget's tasks', *Psych. Mon.*, 76, 36 (whole No.555).

GOTTFRIED, A.W., and BRADY, N. (1975) 'Interrelationship between and correlates of psychometric and Piagetian scales of sensorimotor intelligence', *Dev. Psych.*, 11, 3, 379—387.

GOUIN-DECARIE, T. (1965) *Intelligence and affectivity in early childhood*. New York: International Universities Press.

GRATCH, G., and LANDERS, W.F. (1967) 'A partial replication of Piaget's study of infant's object concepts', paper presented at the meeting of the Society for Research in Child Development, N.Y. March.

GRATCH, G., and LANDERS, W. (1971) 'Stage IV of Piaget's theory of infant's object concepts: a longitudinal study', *Child Developm.*, 42, 359- 372.

GRATCH, G., APPEL, K.J., EVANS, W.F., LECOMPTE, G.K., and WRIGHT, N.A. (1974) 'Piaget' stage IV object concept error: evidence of forgetting or object conception?', *Child Developm.*, 45, 71—77.

GREEN, B.F.A. (1956) 'A method of scalogram analysis using summary statistics', *Psychomet.*, 21, 79—88.

GREENFIELD, P.M., NELSON, K., and SALTZMAN, E. (1972) 'The development of rulebound strategies for manipulating seriated cups: a parallel between action and grammar', *Cog. Psychol.*, 3, 291—310.

GRUBER, H.E., GIRGUS, J.S., and BANUAZIZI, A. (1971) 'The development of object permanence in the cat', *Dev. Psych.*, 4, 9—15.

HANES, M.L. (1974) 'Cognition and the acquisition of selected fuction words in poverty children', *Diss. Abst.*, 34, 8, 4479A—5379A, (4925A). Xerox University Microfilms.

HARRIS, P.L. (1973) 'Perseverative errors in search by young infants', *Child Developm.*, 44, 28–33.

HARRIS, P.L. (1974) 'Perseverative search at a visibly empty place by young infants', *J. Exp. Child Psych.*, 18, 535–542.

HARRIS, P.L. (1975) 'The development of search and object permanence during infancy', Personal communication.

HAZLITT, V. (1930) 'Children's thinking', *Brit. J. Psych.*, 20, 354–61.

HEIDER, F. (1958) *The Psychology of Interpersonal Relations*. New York: Wiley.

HUGHES, M.M. (1965) A four-year longitudinal study of the growth of logical thinking in a group of secondary modern schoolboys. MEd thesis, University of Leeds.

HUNT, J. McV. (1961) *Intelligence and Experience*. New York: Ronald.

HUNT, J. McV. (1969) 'The impact and limitations of the giant of developmental psychology'. In: ELKIND, D. and FLAVELL, J.H. (Eds.), *Studies in Cognitive Development*. New York: Oxford University Press.

HUNT, J. McV. (1972) 'Sequential order and plasticity in early psychological development'. Paper presented at the Jean Piaget Society's Second Annual Symposium, Temple University, Philadelphia.

INHELDER, B. (1962) 'Some aspects of Piaget's genetic approach to cognition'. In: KESSEN, W. and KUHLMAN, C. (Eds.), *Thought in the Young Child*. Report of a conference on intellective development with particular attention to the work of Piaget. Monographs of the Society for Research in Child Development, 27, 2, serial 83, 19–34.

INHELDER, B. (1972) 'Information processing tendencies in recent experiments in cognitive learning – empirical studies'. In: FARNHAM-DIGGORY, S. (Ed.), *Information Processing in Children*. New York: Academic Press.

INHELDER, B., SINCLAIR, H. and BOVET, M. (1974) *Learning and the Development of Cognition*. Cambridge, Mass.: Harvard University Press. (French edition PUF France, 1974).

ISAACS, N. (1950) 'Critical notice: Traité de logique – Essai de logistique operatoire by J. Piaget', *Brit. J. Psych.*, 42, 85–88.

JURASCHEK, W.A. (1975) 'The performance of prospective teachers on certain Piagetian tasks', *Diss. Abst.*, 35, 9, 5581A–6281A (5989–A).

KAGAN, J., and KOGAN, N. (1970) 'Individuality and cognitive performance'. In: MUSSEN, P.H. (Ed.), *Carmichael's Manual of child psychology*. Volume One. New York: Wiley.

KAPLAN, J.D. (1967) Teaching number conservation to disadvantaged children. Unpublished Doctoral Dissertation, Columbia University, New York.

KARMILOFF-SMITH, A., and INHELDER, B. (1975) ' "If you want to get ahead, get a theory" ', *Cognition*, 3, 3, 195–212.

KATZ, J.J. and FODOR, J.A. (1963) 'The structures of a semantic theory', *Language*, 39, 2, 170–210.

KELLY, M.R. (1970) 'Some aspects of conservation of quantity and length in Papua and New Guinea in relation to language, sex and years at school'. Territory of Papua and New Guinea. *Journ. Educ.*, 55–60.

KIMBALL, R. (1973) 'The teaching and understanding of formal operations'. Paper delivered to the Third Annual Conference on 'Piaget and the Helping Professions'. Children's Hospital, Los Angeles.

KIMBALL, R. (1975) 'Spontaneity and formal operations'. Paper presented at the Fifth Annual Conference on Piaget and the Helping Professions, sponsored jointly by the U.A.P. Project at Children's Hospital, Los Angeles and University of Southern California.

KING, W.L., and SEEGMILLER, B. (1973) 'Performance of 14-to-22-month-old black, firstborn male infants on two tests of cognitive development: The Bayley Scales and the Infant, Psychological Development Scale', *Dev. Psych.*, 8, 317–326.

KOHLBERG, L. (1972) 'Development as the aim of Education', *Harv. Educ. Rev.*, 42, 449–496.

KOPP, C.B. (1973) 'Neuromuscular integrity and use of sensory motor schemes'. Paper presented at the biennial meeting of the Soc. for Res. in Child Development, Philadelphia, March.

KOPP, C.B., O'CONNOR, M. and FINGER, I. (1975) 'Task characteristics and a stage six sensorimotor problem', *Child Developm.*, 46, 569–73.

KOPP, C.B., SIGMAN, M., and PARMELEE, A.H. (1973) 'Ordinality and sensory-motor series', *Child Developm.*, 44, 821–823.

KOPP, C.B., SIGMAN, M., and PARMELEE, A.H. (1974) 'Longitudinal study of sensorimotor development', *Dev. Psych.*, 10, 5, 687–695.

KOSLOWSKI, B., and BRUNER, J. (1972) 'Learning to use a lever', *Child Developm.*, 43, 790–799.

KRAMER, J.A., HILL, K.T., and COHEN, L.B. (1975) 'Infant's development of object permanence: a refined methodology and new evidence for Piaget's hypothesized ordinality', *Child Developm.*, 46, 149–155.

LABOV, W. (1970) 'The study of language in its social context', *Studium Generale*, 23, 66—84.

LANDERS, W.F.C. (1971) 'Effects of differential experience on infants' performance in a Piagetian stage IV, object-concept task', *Dev. Psych.*, 5, 48—54.

LANGER, J. (1969a) *Theories of Development*. New York: Holt, Rinehart and Winston.

LANGER, J. (1969b) 'Disequilibrium as a source of development'. In: MUSSEN, P.H., LANGER, J. and COVINGTON, M. (Eds.) *Trends and Issues in Developmental Psychology*. New York: Holt, Rinehart and Winston.

LANGER, J. (1975) 'Interactional aspects of cognitive organization', *Cognition*, 3 (1) 9—28.

LAURENDEAU, M. and PINARD, A. (1962) *Causal Thinking in the Child*. New York: International University Press.

LECOMPTE, G.K., and GRATCH, G. (1972) 'Violation of a rule as a method of diagnosing infants' levels of object concept', *Child Developm.*, 43, 385—96.

LONGOBARDI, E.T., and WOLFF, P.A. (1973) 'A comparison of motoric and verbal responses on a Piagetian rate-time task', *Child Developm.*, 44, 433—437.

LOVELL, K. (1968) 'Experimental Foundations'. In: *Piaget in Perspective*. Papers read at a conference of Sussex University, School of Education, 1—12, April 5—6.

LUNZER, E.A. (1968) *The Regulation of Behaviour: Development in Learning*. Vol. 1. London: Staples Press.

LURIA, A.R. (1959) 'The directive function of speech in development and dissolution part I', *Word*, 15, 341—352.

MATHENY, A.P., Jr. (1975) 'Twins: concordance for Piagetian-equivalent items derived from the Bayley Mental Test', *Developm. Psych.*, 11, 2, 224—227.

McCALL, R.B., HOGARTY, P.S., and HURLBURT, N. (1972) 'Transitions in infant sensorimotor development and the prediction of childhood in IQ', *Amer. Psych.*, 27, 728—748.

MILLER, D., COHEN, L.B., and HILL, K.T. (1969) 'A test of Piaget's notions on object concept development in the sensorimotor period', Paper delivered at biennial meeting of the Soc. for Res. on Child Developm., Santa Monica, California.

MILLER, D.J., COHEN, L.B., and HILL, K.T. (1970) 'A methodological investigation of Piaget's theory of object concept development in the sensory-motor period', *J. Exp. Child Psych.*, 9, 1, 59—85.

MODGIL, S. (1974) *Piagetian Research: A Handbook of Recent*

Studies. Windsor: National Foundation for Educational Research.
MOERK, E.L. (1975) 'Piaget's research as applied to the explanation of language development', *Merr.-Palm. Quart.*, 21, 3, 151–69.
MORRIS, C.W. (1946) *Signs, Language and Behaviour.* New York: Prentice-Hall.
MOUNOUD, P. and BOWER, T.G.R. (1975) 'Conservation of weight in infants', *Cognition*, 3, 1, 29–40.
NICOLICH, L. McCUNE, and RAPH, J.B. (1975) 'A longitudinal study of representational play in relation to spontaneous imitation and development of multi-word utterances', personal communication.
NOLEN, P. (1975) 'Acquisition of logical codes: forms, content and language', Personal communication. Also, paper presented at the Conference on Culture and Communication, Philadelphia: Temple University, March.

OGDEN, C.K. and RICHARDS, I.A. (1923) *The Meaning of Meaning.* New York: Harcourt, Brace and World.
OLSEN, B.A., CROSS, H.A., and VAUGHTER, R.M. (1966) Apparatus note: a modified WGTA for children', *Psychon. Sc.*, 5, 319.

PALFREY, C.F. (1972) 'Piaget's questions to young children: an analysis of their structure and content', *Educ. Rev.*, 24, 2, 122–131.
PARASKEVOPOULOS, J., and HUNT, J. McV. (1971) 'Object construction and imitation under differing conditions of rearing', *J. Gen. Psych.*, 119, 301–321.
PARSONS, C. (1960) 'Inhelder and Piaget's "The Growth of Logical Thinking", II, a Logician's viewpoint', *Brit. J. Psych.*, 51, 1, 75–84.
PASCUAL-LEONE, J. (1975, in press) 'A view of cognition from a formalist's perspective'. In: RIEGEL, K.F. (Ed.), *Current issues in developmental psychology.* Basel: S. Karger.
PEEL, E.A. (1960) *The Pupil's Thinking.* London: Oldbourne.
PEEL, E.A. (1971) *The Nature of Adolescent Judgement.* London: Staples.
PEIRCE, C.S. (1932) *Collected Papers of Charles Sanders Peirce.* Vol. 2. Cambridge Mass: Harvard Univ. Press.
PELUFFO, N. (1967) 'Culture and cognitive problems', *Int. J. Psych.*, 2, 187–198.
PIAGET, J. (For all Piaget References in this volume, please refer to 'Piaget's Major Works', pp. 25–32.
PINARD, A., and LAURENDEAU, M. (1969) ' "Stage" in Piaget's cognitive developmental theory: exegesis of a concept'. In: ELKIND, D. and FLAVELL, J.H. (Eds.) *Studies in Cognitive Development: Essays in Honour of Jean Piaget.* New York: Oxford

University Press.
PUFALL, P.B., SHAW, R.E., and SYDRAL-LASKY, A. (1973) 'Development of number conservation: an examination of some predictions from Piaget's Stage analysis and equilibration model', *Child Developm.*, 44, 21—27.

RIEGEL, K.F. (1973) 'Dialectic operations: the final period of cognitive development', *Human Developm.*, 16, 346—370.
ROBERTS, G.C., and BLACK, K.N. (1972) 'The effect of naming and object permanence on toy preferences', *Child Developm.*, 43, 958—68.
ROSENBLATT, D. (1975) 'Play and language: the development of representational thought in infancy', personal communication. Also, Paper presented at the Annual BPS Conference, September, York University.
RUMBAUGH, D.M. (1968) 'The learning and sensory capacities of the squirrel monkey in phylogenetic perspective'. In: ROSENBLUM, L.A. and COOPER, R.W. (Eds.). *The squirrel monkey.* New York: Academic Press.
RUMBAUGH, D.M., and McCORMICK, C. (1967) 'The learning skills of primates: a comparative study of apes and monkeys'. In: STARCK, D. SCHNEIDER, R. and KUHN, H.S. (Eds.), *Progress in primatology.* Stuttgart: Fischer.

SCHOFIELD, L., and UZGIRIS, I.C. (1969) 'Examining behaviour and the development of the concept of object'. Paper presented at the meeting of the Society for Research in Child Development. Santa Monica, California.
SCHRIER, A.M., HARLOW, H.G., and STOLINITZ, F. (1965) *Behaviour of nonhuman primates.* Vol. 1 and 2. New York: Academic Press.
SELMAN, R.L. (1975) Book Review of 'Thinking Goes to School: Piaget's Theory in Practice', *Harv. Ed. Rev.*, 45, 1, 127—134.
SINCLAIR, H. (1971) 'Sensorimotor action patterns as a condition for the acquisition of syntax'. In: HUXLEY, R. and INGRAM, E. (Eds.). *Language acquisition: models and methods.* New York: Academic Press.
SINCLAIR, H. (1972) 'Some comments on Fodor's "Reflections on L.S. Vygotsky's thought and language" ', *Cogn.*, 1, 4, 317—318.
SLOBIN, D.I. (1973) 'Cognitive prerequisites for the development of grammar'. In: FERGUSON, C.A. and SLOBIN, D.I. (Eds.) *Studies of Child Language Development.* New York: Holt, Rinehart and Winston.
SMILLIE, D. (1972) 'Piaget's constructionist theory', *Human*

Developm., 15, 171—186.

SMITH, D.A. (1970) The construction of the object. Unpublished PhD thesis, Leeds University.

STEINER, G. (1974) 'On the psychological reality of cognitive structures: a tentative synthesis of Piaget's and Bruner's theories, *Child Developm.*, 45, 891—99.

STEPHENS, W.B.,   McLAUGHLIN, A.,   MILLER, C.K.   and GLASS, G.V. (1972) 'Factorial structure of selected psycho-educational measures and Piagetian reasoning assessments', *Dev. Psych.*, 6, 2, 343.

STEWIN, L.L. and MARTIN, J. (1974) 'The developmental stages of L.S. Vygotsky and J. Piaget: a comparison. *Alberta J. Ed. Res.* 20, 348—62.

TOMLINSON-LEASEY, C. (1972) 'Formal operations in females from 11 to 54 years of age', *Dev. Psycholog.*, 6, 364.

TURSI, P.A. (1973) 'Exposition, analysis and implication of selected presuppositions inherent in Piaget's theory', *Diss. Abst.*, 34, 2, 453A—927A, (673A), Xerox University Microfilms.

UZGIRIS, I.C. 1967) 'Ordinality in the development of schemas for relating to objects'. In: HELLMUTH, J. (Ed.). *Exceptional Infant.* Vol. 1: 'The normal infant'. New York: Bruner/Mazel.

UZGIRIS, I.C. (1973) 'Patterns of cognitive development in infancy', *Merr.-Palm. Quart.*, 19, 181—204.

UZGIRIS, I.C., and HUNT, J. McV. (1966) 'An instrument for measuring infant psychological development'. Progress report of work supported by US Public Health Grant 5—K6—MN—18, 567 (Hunt), MH—07347, and MH—08468.

UZGIRIS, I.C., and HUNT, J. McV. (1968) 'An instrument for assessing infant psychological development'. Paper presented at the 18th intern. Congress of Psychology, Moscow.

UZGIRIS, I.C., and HUNT, J. McV. (1974) *Assessment in Infancy: ordinal scales of psychological development*. Urbana: University of Illinois Press.

VAUGHTER, R.M., SMOTHERMAN, W., and ORDY, J.M. (1972) 'Development of object permanence in the infant squirrel monkey', *Dev. Psych.*, 7, 1, 34—38.

VINH BANG (1971) 'The psychology of Jean Piaget and its relevance to Education'. Cited in RUSK, B. (Ed.), *Alternatives in Education.* London University Press.

VON-HIPPEL, C.L. (1972) 'Piaget's work in early child development as it relates to Chomskian Psycholinguistics'. *Diss. Abst.*, Order No.

72—15032, Xerox University Micro-films.

WACHS, T.D. (1970) 'Report on the utility of a Piaget-based infant scale with older retarded children', *Dev. Psych.*, 2, 3, 449.

WACHS, T.D., UZGIRIS, I., and HUNT, J. McV. (1967) 'Cognitive development in infants of different age levels and from different environmental backgrounds'. Paper presented at the biennial meeting of the Soc. for Res. in Child Development, New York.

WACHS, T., UZGIRIS, I., and HUNT, J. McV. (1971) 'Cognitive development in infants of different age levels and from different environmental backgrounds: an explanatory investigation', *Merr.-Palm. Quart.*, 17, 283—317.

WAITE, J.B. (1975) 'A study comparing college science students' performance on Piagetian type tasks, including cross-cultural comparisons', *Diss. Absts.*, March, 35, 9, 5581A—6281A (5954—A).

WALKERDINE, W., and SINHA, C. (1975) 'The internal triangle: language, reasoning and the social context'. Personal communication. Also to be published in MAKOVA, I. (Ed.), *Language in the social context*. John Wiley and Sons Limited (in press).

WALLACE, J.G. (1973) 'Class-inclusion performance in children: information-processing theories and experimental studies'. Paper read at the British Psychological Society Conference, Liverpool University, Easter.

WEBB, R.A., MASSAR, B., and NADOLNY, T. (1972) 'Information and strategy in the young child's search for hidden objects', *Child Developm.*, 43, 91—104.

WECHSLER, D. (1949) *Wechsler Intelligence Scale for Children*. New York: Psychological Corporation.

WEINREB, N., and BRAINERD, C.J. (1975) 'A developmental study of Piaget's groupement model of the emergence of speed and time concepts', *Child Develop.*, 46, 176—185.

WEINRICH, U. (1963) 'On the semantic structure of language'. In: GREENBERG, J. (Ed.) *Universals of Language*. Cambridge, Mass.: MIT Press.

WERE, K. (1968) A survey of the thought process of New Guinean secondary students. Unpublished MEd thesis, Adelaide University.

WILDEN, A. (1973) *System and Structure*. London: Tavistock.

WILLERMAN, L. and FIELDER, M.F. (1974) 'Infant performance and intellectual precocity', *Child Developm.*, 45, 483—86.

WILSON, R.S. (1970) 'Bloodtyping and twin zygosity', *Hum. Hered.*, 20, 30—56.

WISE, K.L., WISE, L.A., and ZIMMERMANN, R.R. (1974) 'Piagetian object performance in the infant rhesus monkey', *Dev. Psych.*, 10, 3, 429—437.

WOODWARD, M. (1972) 'Problem-solving strategies of young children', *J. Child Psych. Psychiatr.*, 13, 11—24.

WOODWARD, M., and HUNT, M.R. (1972) 'Exploratory studies of early cognitive development', *Brit J. Ed. Psych.*, 248—59.

INDEX

Aebli, H., 51
Appel, K. J., 122, 124, 132
Apostel, L., 48
Arlin, P. K., 45, 46
Athey, I., 64
Atwood, G., 60, 70, 71

Babska, Z., 121
Banuazizi, A., 125, 134
Bart, W. M., 48, 56, 69
Bayley, N., 107, 139, 140
Beard, R. M., 64
Begelman, D. A., 52
Beilin, H., 51
Bell, S. M., 120, 121, 122, 147
Berzonsky, M. D., 47
Beth, E. W., 27
Bever, T. G., 60
Biaggio, A., 60, 70, 71
Binet, A., 18
Birns, B., 108, 121
Black, K. N., 37, 123
Blanchard, E. B., 60
Bleuler, E., 18
Bloom, B., 141
Bovet, M., 92
Bower, T. G. R., 111, 112, 115, 116,
     117, 118, 120, 122, 126, 127,
     129, 142, 143, 145
Boyle, D. G., 53, 65, 72, 73
Brady, N., 117
Braine, M. D. S., 51
Brainerd, C., 50
Brehim, J., 71
Broughton, J., 115, 127
Brown, I. E., 118
Brown, R. W., 60, 91
Brumer, S., 53, 74
Bruner, J., 39, 52, 109, 141
Bryant, P., 111, 118
Bukatko, D., 111
Bühler, C., 78
Burt, C., 18
Butterworth, G., 117
Buss, A. R., 55, 108

Carlsmith, J., 71
Casati, I., 108, 109, 137, 138
Case, R., 67, 68, 74, 75, 76, 77

Cassel, R. N., 61, 78
Catalogue (J. Piaget Archives), 99,
     100
Cattell, R. B., 88
Cellérier, G., 62
Chafe, W. L., 59
Charlesworth, W. R., 122, 147
Chomsky, N., 57, 101
Claparède, E., 19
Coan, R. W., 88
Coffman, B. S. P., 110, 130
Cohen, L., 109, 120, 121, 137, 139
Corman, H., 107, 121, 137, 140, 141
Cross, H. A., 147

Daehler, M. W., 111
Daele, L. Van Den., 56
Dasen, P., 37, 43
Décaire, T. G., 37, 121, 137, 138,
     145
Dirlam, D. K., 56, 57, 79, 80, 81
Dodwell, P. C., 47
Donaldson, M., 62
Dudek, S. Z., 50, 88
Dyer, G. B., 50, 88

Edwards, D., 110
Einstein, A., 20
Elkind, D., 17, 64
Escalona, S., 107, 121, 137, 140, 141
Evans, W. F., 123, 124, 132

Festinger, L., 71
Fiedler, M., 109
Finger, I., 109, 136, 137
Flavell, J. H., 50, 51, 55, 56, 88, 89,
     121.
Fodor, J. A., 59
Freud, S., 18
Furby, L., 69, 90
Furth, H., 64, 72, 73

Gagné, R., 67, 68, 69, 90
Galanter, E., 52
Gander, M., 69, 90
Gardner, H., 56, 79
Gascon, J., 62
Gilmore, S., 51

Ginsburg, H. J., 51, 118, 131, 132
Girgus, J., 125, 134
Golden, M., 108, 121
Goodnow, J., 45
Gottfried, A., 117
Gratch, G., 122, 123, 124, 132, 145, 147
Green, B. F., 108, 138
Greenfield, P. M., 120, 141, 144
Gruber, H., 125, 134

Hanes, M. L., 58, 91
Harlow, H., 147
Harris, P. L., 116, 117, 133, 135, 136
Hays, J. R., 57, 79, 81
Hazlitt, V., 47
Heider, F., 60
Hill, B., 24
Hill, K. T., 109, 120, 121, 137, 139
Hogarty, P. S., 107
Hughes, M. M., 45
Hunt, J. McV., 38, 55, 107, 108, 119, 137, 139, 140
Hurlburt, N., 107

Inhelder, B., *passim*
Isaacs, N., 48

Juraschek, W. A., 45

Kagan, J., 55
Kaplan, J., 55
Karmiloff-Smith, A., 60, 92, 93, 94
Katz, J., 59
Kelly, M., 45
Kimball, R., 45, 48
King, W. L., 108, 139
Kohlberg, L., 65
Kogan, N., 55
Kopp, C., 108, 109, 117, 121, 136, 137, 138, 139
Koslowski, B., 109
Kramer, J., 120, 139

Labov, W., 60
Landers, W., 122, 145, 147
Langer, J., 57, 94, 95
Laurendeau, M., 50, 88
LeCompte, G., 123, 124, 132
Lézine, I., 108, 109, 137, 138, 141
Longobardi, E. T., 111
Lovell, K., 44
Lunzer, E. A., 41, 42
Luria, A. R., 122, 123

Martin, J., 57
Maslow, A., 78, 79
Massar, B., 123, 148
Matheny, A. P., 107, 140
McCall, R., 107
McCormick, C., 147
Mendez, G., 57, 79
Michal, D. Z., 57, 79
Miller, D. J., 121, 137, 139
Mischel, T., 51
Modgil, S., 23, 43, 45, 112, 121, 122, 123, 145
Moerk, E. L., 59, 60
Moore, M. K., 115, 127
Morris, C. W., 59
Mounoud, P., 111, 112, 142, 143
Mussen, P. H., 36

Nadolny, T., 123, 148
Nelson, K., 120, 144
Nicolich, L. McCune, 109, 141
Nolen, P., 45, 49

O'Connor, M., 109, 136, 137
Ogden, C., 59
Olsen, B., 147
Olver, R. R., 141
Opitz, D., 57, 79
Ordy, J., 125, 126, 147, 148

Paivio, A., 81
Palfrey, C. F., 51, 95, 96
Palm, J., 57, 79
Paraskevopoulos, J., 38, 108
Parmelee, A. H., 108, 121, 137, 138
Pascual-Leone, J., 67, 68, 77, 78
Paterson, J. G., 115, 116, 126
Peel, E. A., 43, 45
Peirce, C. S., 59
Peluffo, N., 45
Piaget, J., *passim*
Pinard, A., 50, 88
Pribram, K. H., 52
Price, K., 60
Pufall, P.B., 47

Raph, J., 72, 73
Raph, J. B., 109, 141
Richards, I. A., 59
Riegel, K. F., 61, 97
Ripple, R. E., 72
Roberts, G. C., 37, 123
Rockcastle, V., 72
Rosenblatt, D., 109, 143

Royce, J. R., 55, 108
Rumbaugh, D. M., 147

Saltzman, E., 120
Schofield, L., 147
Schrier, A. M., 147
Schwebel, M., 72, 73
Seegmiller, B., 108, 139
Selman, R., 66
Shaw, R., 47
Sigman, M., 108, 121, 137, 138
Simpson, S. C., 60, 70, 71
Sinclair, H., 31, 32, 58, 92, 141
Sinha, C., 62
Slobin, D., 60
Smillie, D., 119, 145
Smith, M. B., 48, 56, 69
Smotherman, W., 125, 126, 147, 148
Steiner, G., 51, 57
Steinfeld, G., 52
Stephens, W. B., 45
Stewin, L., 57
Stollnitz, F., 147
Syrdal-Lasky, A., 47
Szeminska, A., 19, 20, 26, 27

Tomlinson-Keasey, C., 45
Tursi, P. A., 98

Uzgiris, I. C., 37, 47, 107, 108, 115,
   119, 137, 139, 140, 146, 147

Vaughter, R. M., 125, 126, 147, 148
Vinh-Bang, 65
Von Bertalanffy, 98
Von Hippel, C. L. S., 57, 100
Vygotsky, L. S., 57, 58

Wachs, T. D., 37, 72, 73, 108
Waite, J. B., 45
Walkerdine, V., 62
Wallace, J., 49, 52
Webb, R., 123, 148
Wegner, G. A., 60, 70, 71
Weinreb, J., 50
Weinreich, U., 59
Were, K., 45
Weschler, D., 88
Wilden, A., 56
Willerman, L., 109
Wilson, R., 140
Wise, K. L., 125, 126, 149, 150
Wise, L. A., 125, 126, 149, 150
Wishart, J. G., 117, 129
Wohlwill, J. F., 50, 55
Wolff, P., 111
Wong, D. L., 118, 131, 132
Woodward, M., 38
Wright, N. A., 124, 132

Zimmermann, R. R., 125, 126, 149,
   150